The White Basket

Dr. Nathaniel Henry Fox

The White Basket

Table of Contents:

Introduction
Chapter 1: The universe
Chapter 2: Political habit
Chapter 3: The Borat of Uzbekistan
Chapter 4: AI and interrogative development
Chapter 5: Insects from Afghanistan
Chapter 6: Advancing political theory amidst clock failure
Chapter 7: Aliens and the skies
Chapter 8: Reaching out
Chapter 9: Self-worth
Chapter 10: The bad apples of radio astronomy
Chapter 11: The instigation of a legend against the almighty
Chapter 12: Merry Christmas
Acknowledgments

The White Basket

Introduction:

The wind begins its torrent across the fields of the flattened landscape. The fields have been sewn and the families are moving away from the vacant lot. Aloneness is the safe harbour from the sanctimonious repositioning required through the day. The gift is book by book a story of openness and ease, this one being one of them. In the cold we are tight and cold together. In the heat we are exposed and enchant to be cooler. May this be then for all seasons.

There is a difference in people when the weather turns that we notice slightly unusual characteristics of one another, yet so cold as we may live in the winter our hearts go to edges of the universe to find peace. We hope with much solidarity that the heat stays bustling that our plight as countrymen may continue to resolve. We find that the air is better breathed when there are fresh ideas for us to hold as some invention, which is at our fingertips. What else we need, we look to the market, there where there is a development. The skies are the boundaries.

Imagine this work for yourself again that the edges of the galaxies are open to us and that the inviting presence of the universe is with us always. Keep in your spirit that that Minerval inner-yearning for truth to this day is the warmth in the legs upon the bed to then sleep, that we may dream to the great universe even. The growing openness of the moment can threaten us by way of distance from the book. Thus, keep *The White Basket* close to stay warm or

The White Basket

near to the body in the heat that it may bring shade and natural coolness.

This book is a mix of real-world experiences and varied political musings as well as unabashed legal theory to do with Luciferianism and its modern linguistic impact upon the theosophist and scientist. From the perspective of the modern individual, *The White Basket* brings to the reader a new way of seeing the modern world with its emerging challenges. It is a work for the ages and challenges to a demanding standard to be but a quick to publish and short read amidst our evolving social readiness and pulse-driven social media. It is my hope it suits the backpack well, that the winter timeframe wherein it has been written does not claim the life that a fresh perspective and optimism about survival does not emerge instead. Effort. Standard. These are the aims of *The White Basket*.

During the Trump Administration, life as an American has changed. Media outpourings are fast and overwhelming. Americans are searching for clarity and struggle to stay focused amidst world dealings and a withdraw of American presence from the regions of and about Syria. How I've found my own sense amidst heat and cold is by challenging the reader to be expressive to an audience over the course of many works their own. I encourage the audience to publish books that they may better defend their families. And by way of communication, I have learned much from my president to do right and

The White Basket

challenge the perspectives of authority, his own included. I hope this work inspires the reader to be more expressive and inclusive to do with international topics, that it may suit well a strong tool to examine and engage with others about our Great Earth. Though I struggle within my state to stay right with my family and not frighten them in my dire stubbornness to publish, it is my aim to strive toward peace. I aim to build a canonical presence about my writings that my country is better defended and that parties international can be examined from a fresh and emerging American perspective. I contend to the health of the lives of those struggling with insanity and other mental illness and it is I contest to my own mistreatment within the healthcare system to have made inappropriate assertions regarding the scope of my intelligence. My embrace of the works of Aleister Crowley and legal theory to do with Luciferianism have left me at odds with churches and the Christians within my family. Perhaps there can be no other way than continue to write.

It is my hope that with the addition of this work to my collection of publications that more tools can be added for the reader should there be some modern revival of such topics as spiritualism and theosophy, asserting force in print to the church body as a whole. To consider the life as isolated, we will be hampered by the developing world, thus I am to free the bond of restriction in myself somehow whilst maintaining due course with the arts. I must persist

The White Basket

that there remaining beyond my death is a collection of works worth the endearing study. Meanwhile, I thrive.

The White Basket

Chapter 1: The universe

The voice of the universe has broadcasted throughout the cosmos some manifestation of value and importance to life. The life we have is our being and the importance of that being is often graded to the material resolute that should I just feel some degree of comfort, it is so simply there is an everlasting sense of peace. But so much hard work has been made with effort that to be simply present, aware of the moment, we are unfit to lead and must harness the powers of our memory and muscle. We must be optimistic and push hard to win at the edges of the day.

In our winter it is cold to the extent this cold is dangerous. We are surrounded by the angst of the day, the forecasting event of our lifetime impeding our journey out and into the world where we would stretch out before the sun our toes and fingers. There is little resolute change in the openness to the cold that spiritually there must be a challenge. And howsoever plain as day as the events may be, there is the payment of the Mercury for its tithes to Saturn; the movement of the ephemeris is more of a subtle nomenclature to our tasks at hand than an impediment. But it is in the Mercury that there is the resolute factor for change which has been that bad habit of the hatter, who is mad to his days though he finds use in the elements.

There is an open flame to the endearing path of the wanderer who journeys so far into the universe, there is life as it is, but with a twist. The life we lead is side-by-side to

The White Basket

some other drift through the star pattern, but aye, there is that journey that has strayed from the closest we could have kindled; peace to the warmth and the circuit we know as health that we are of touch to the summer, some degree cooler for pleasure - a madness.

Contemplate the bickering spirit in the cold and should it be warm that we read for the pain of the travesty we have remembered, we are felt to resolve to circumstances to embrace some degree of individuality. And it is there is that heavy weight to resolve the body to tension for the betterment of the tactile flavours, that we may feel the body in its warmth. We want warmth and we want the cool. We want these elements to transform some degree of power for us that the winds move by our will as we breath with control. There is that fanciful martial arts to the casual weather modification en local; in our perseverance and studies of the reality before us, through our meditations and striving to bend law to focus, there is that will to change this moment to our casual fitness. Should we fail to encapsulate a powerful enough trigger in the frigidness that our limbs do not crisp, there is that warmth that is knife-edge hot. For the study of the stars to commence, let us prepare our basket of a wilful power that we can beckon to push and pull through the body that we are saved to sleep a common restfulness and attain to a martial quietude.

That we have confronted the cold and our nails have grown to considerable length under the pressures of

The White Basket

the winter, find that the year-long seasonal attitude is but a trimming, that to trim back the nail there is that recognition that one is able to form words and that we are not to be stopped from hallucinating our brave English language too by a cuticle. Should our knuckles form to a violence, we must be at least somewhat prepared to confront the turmoil of our open games with the universe. Before we would do that, to take up arms against the state, it is best to engage with the hands to find resoluteness there. A farmer is none without his almanac.

Cut the hair. It grows long into the face and it must be cut that we are well groomed for the intermediary spaces where there is confrontation with the public. We must seek to get along with the public and close tightly that martial bond that allows for us free entrance into the public domain. Speech should be natural. It is best that we practice our speech when alone that our natural insanity fuses with our desire to act. It is in our aloneness we find opportunity to gamble on our material destiny, that we will or will not succeed whence public speaking and action takes place. It is not unnatural to be without worry for the hair, though it has been sorted out, the cut ends hopefully not traded to the market. Donation of the hair is for a different politician altogether, one who is quite astounded by their hair. We have done away with it.

Do not rely on always-washed clothing as the winter is costly and trips to the market could be fewer. Remember those articles of clothing that are about the

The White Basket

house and cling somewhat to the dirty environment. It can be helpful to hand-wash certain delicates like scarves. Do you have a scarf? Is there not a magical favourite in the tradition of the elementary householder? At least one fine scarf is recommended for the spiritualist in the keeping of his estate. Aristocracy must not dodder to the whimsical fantasy of the sick anthroposophical illness of the warmth of the Spanish house.

Perhaps it is your autumn and we are in winter, which would be like Mars or Jupiter, even Io. Moments on Saturn are quite luxurious in the fall but you need not dress but a disproportionate comfort to your season to be in better alignment with the spiritual. Even in summer, I feel for the lessons of winter. This is part of *The White Basket*.

A gentle weave to the story, what is prepared is one's home. Clean up the home and leave some things strewn about that there is something in the way to be seen and otherwise recognised by the body. And perhaps it is to the liking that there is some habit? Perhaps, a smoker? Then enjoy that. Take some time after exposing objects to the openness of the environment to celebrate. Refrain from intoxication.

Of course there is the other aspect to martial arts to say, "No, I don't want to do that." Then do that. Make that an object and take that to the market. Engage with someone in public without smoking perhaps? On my estate, smoking is most welcome.

The White Basket

Perhaps the market is a fanciful effort or too dangerous to reach toward as a goal for the day? It could be so. No matter the rural jurisdiction, plan in some way to engage with the public and worry about the matters that come to mind. Become intentional in the privacy to voice concerns about personal ethics in some way than verbal should there be some disturbance of the mouth from the weather. Mull over the details of the things at hand and pressure the body to perform while holding in mind those politics most essential to remembering the basic components of our basket. Your basket is unique, though there is propaganda about the matter.

In developing one's attitude about the season, it is not unusual to prefer heat from cold, nor cold from heat; there is a retribution of sorts that follows the heart of a being who is injured by the nefariousness of our season. It is to bring about a peace and yet to retain power - this is a sort of madness we will confront throughout our lifetime and we can very easily use politics to dispute the matters most psychological from physical. Most assuredly, we must be well-kept and remain presentable to the public, else there will be doubts as to our prowess as to how it fits for our longterm progress. Remember the market and that we are well-kept.

Chapter 2: Political habit

The White Basket

It is not unusual to be political with one's habit. Let us begin anew with the goal of politics in mind. It can be that few people want to engage in talk with the public to do with politics, but it is the responsibility of the grown adult to master his or her estate. They must navigate in public presentation with the awkward gait that comes with being an accomplished martial artist. Should one present the gait to be unusual or too aggressive, one will lose face with the market. Do not strike out at the public to do some injustice to them. Enact the politics of the feature to the likeness that one is standing in a mirror waiting to be walked-away; there is no moment of collapse. Rarely do the hands touch in public. It is in the scope of our political theory presented that the hands are not to be touching, that there is no inner prayer resolution for the coward who is humbled at the market. May the intricacies of the basket form to the likeness that prayer is reserved for the home rather than public.

How are the legs? Is it that the season permits comfort or is it not duly recognised that the individual must perform to their martial honesty about the weather? Find solace in the legs. Perceive where the footwear is in the household. Is there a panic in the back? Find organisation in the footwear. But let us not fall to the entire day sorting that which touches the feet. Can you touch the feet from the waist, bending forward?

Good. Perfection in the form is sometimes expressed as several shoes not quite measuring a common

The White Basket

lace length, that all the laces seem attached and this forms a type of fungal computer the English will go mad for - for ours we have defunct by proxy. Let us not match a shoe by accident.

It can be detestable to want to eat and shower at the same time, that to ingest food while showering one may be interpreted as marking time for the barbiturate without weights. Has the centre of the chest been lost to Epstein Barr for the play of the Oaspey dentist in his aesthetic loss for English company? It is in Lucifer that the algorithm of a perfect beauty is rare but delicate, laughable decipherment of the affect leaving one leathery and overworked, a hanging image of the inner residue left over from illumination of the intellect when time was all matter resolute. The time and the universe are waiting. In the English fever to rise to the lack of portability of the Big Ben and given the Time Lord's addition to Earth another leap-second, it is the prepared man who needs but a fine watch to be that minute fast that he has adopted the proper algebra for the House of Commons. Mathematics it has faired, has come to evolve.

For the secular approach to a Church environment, there is nothing like being able to open up on the expanse of the universe in its recent accreditation for being intact yet resilient enough to expand a little-zipper quickly to the larger Russian side of the mountainous fashion. Should one be nought but dishonourable of the fashion one has picked, it is that the advantage for the smaller country is to

The White Basket

demolish the big, that the choices are choices and wins for losses; wellness in examination fitness amidst the Mexican sun.

There is that instigation of the sorrows of suffering that should the reactionary person be careless in his disposition there is but a fascination with the suffering of man and woman that no woman and no man can come together to bring back the bonds that have cried out from elsewhere than from the Luciferian store, so says a maid for Thelema in her bland acceptance of Egypt. And there can be no modern adoption of the modern pyramid without Masonic procession of proper schooling in chemistry and mathematics than to invent an alchemy about the improvisatory triangle surface. I mean to say Virginia is not without her opiate to defend the shores of our mystical law lines drawn to the Ephemeris that Hubbard's recognition of France is any more the clearer. Juris that the common suffragist reject the anaesthetic for the constancy of the bowel. There is sound loss for constitutional argument in the Thelemite without Ma'at in the rhythm of Seshat at this time. The householder in his theosophy must find some defeat the crisis of the opiate even to the extent of theft of idea, that the free taking of cannabis is about for the Irish for our vice president's transgressions into Pelosi's defence of Yeats that she may safely travel to the North. Shame on the Iceland pirate that we are not armed.

The White Basket

One. Two. Three. This is the manifestation of the doubt of the mind. There is an easy way to fail the mathematics of politics and it is in counting to the fingers that notated delicacy that no person can grasp the inner reaching power of attainment without joy in the subtle disgust of one's smell, that personal perfume. There is the subtle hint of the body's natural odour amidst the stench of English reason that there is relief to the vessel should there be detail to duty, which is to deter from the fact. There is resilience in error and one must fight hard to not misguide the surroundings into an open match of hand and foot about all over the place. A war ends and it is in the House of Lords.

To be complaining continually of the sufferings and the misgivings of others, there is that inner resolution to absolve fear and to be granting function to the changes and habits of others. There is a blossoming of a relationship to the universe that can emerge from tightening the body and finding that we are lighter. We can continue to mull at the cavity. Grasp the change of inner resolution that to do work to the body is justifiable restraint against one's inner theosophical teachings. And it is only after recognising the slowly changing face of our inner adversary that we almost know that person to be a resolving force already, that subtle rejection of the Christ about Margaret Fox's spiritualist misgivings to Pennsylvania industry; Grandmother, May She Rest in Peace that I reject Lucifer outright for her and her alone.

The White Basket

In the most immediate sense of the word, it is to absolve into some meaning the sense that 'there is a law and there is a foundation.' *Abjectification* should there be a word to resolve Lucifer, there is the indignant law that beckons to the ordinary countryman. In the ordinary times of irresolute situational awareness, there is a deeply imbibed conundrum wherein the resistance to the force strong is for clerical purposes, abject-strength the resilience of a whole other human phenomenon involving guilt called remorse. It is however to act in due discretion that argument for argument there is thought and every chamber of light generates a noise. It is without simplicity then some argument for the sum of all houses as they clatter bend a room. Anthroposophy has proposed tremendous failures in the Waldorf acceptable standard for adopting the child into his absurd fondness for the orient earlier than recommended by the Chinese.

There is a larger house than the regular place of the market wherefrom one may tithe to words and honour the local citizens whilst theorising the judgement that it may develop well aside and within the basket to do away with verbal rumination altogether. It is the carry-haul that is tricky where there is a mechanical trap in the translations of the Dhammapada for its embrace of Kent's delicate oxen for sustenance and fuel over India. But to separate the instances of the recollections of the mythical path-marker to indicate 'ha-ya' and no "he" to the sound of theoretical chemistry than to blight the fields with some biblical

The White Basket

solution to pain, there is a reason then that the artful dodger doth not rear his ugly head to accept Sartre over Marxist Indian sacrifice for the humanist swami about his orphanage. Be keen to remember in the meditations that there is solace in the evening regardless of the pickings in the day and that no countrymen - it is hoped and shared we know - are against the man in his house to keep bizarre company with the Lord.

There is the concept that a man lives in a country, that he sees the country relative to the power of his objective clarification on the many philosophies of the times of his country's age. He is also aware of other countries should he be a man of such primitive wisdom as to have studied the simplicity of a boundary. There is that acquiescence that to remember the boundary or border between the man's country, there is that concept of civil decision and the possibility of the emergence of conflict within the man's country. It is to sincerely work with the bounds of reason that such a man can conduct himself to leisurely action about the modern estate; even a spiritualist can photograph the manure of the horse to this day and still be resolute to mark change, the range of influence not set to a calculus. The nihilist can emerge in the work habit to accommodate his peace and knowledge of the extraneous other for Camus and cause for a community a grave danger in dealings with money and such a philosopher in his sincere work effort that his country is stable misguides a critical Union with the English.

The White Basket

To be without a country, there is that nameless embrace of the loss of a type of ego associated with pain and the crisis of the inner resolve Vonnegut faced toward the end of his life. There is that mistake one can make to entrain the idea that a state is without a country upon another being at which point there is a possible digression from the substantive nature of the animal form and that there is no keen light for God. Such a natural embrace of the condition as to disassociate from one's apprehension of a country or boundary, there is that risk that the ephemeris can never be apprehended as such a boundary of a sky is omitted from the crisis of possession of one or more things to indicate the possible emergence of a state; the pagan must scythe freely to some strange weeding by the Amish that the scythe raises to arms the berry patch marvellously against the absurdities of the farming German. It is in theory that the world is so large to such an individual who has grown distant from conceptualising a state or boundary that a criminal emerges from within the man's ego as to assault the nation or state according to the modern mystic in their enforcement of prohibition, but only in aims that some absurd philosophy of farming does not emerge within the Seventh-Day Adventist in any some false defence of the rhythms of Norway for strength. There is that criminal justice to be apprehended in the scope of a person or animal who does not respect a boundary, yet there is also an ever-present shadow of love that is cast at the environment when one has meditated to a stateless

The White Basket

consciousness, a consciousness free from the conceptualisation of form or animal spirit that some restriction of meat is no longer tolerated by the Tibetan leadership. It is in the embrace of such form or spirit to do justice to the world against the United States and for that there can be no acceptance of Bön religion to better produce some further tribal inference against women. More to the rites of the matter.

To justify a mathematics, an animal may relate to a concert of animals or creatures within the scope of a state or boundary upon which there is some mark indicating the change of another state with regards apprehended chemical attribution whether this be urine or mere shit. It has been observed that animals substantiate math theory in this way that there is an apprehension of some scope howsoever benign whilst for the intelligent beings of the ways of the world most constitutional, there is that ever pervasive appeal to the science of an idea to justify mathematics in unusual symbolism. It can be that it is *always* in the theory, within the scope of some basic mathematical concept, that an animal has justified the entire scope of mathematics as a whole - by sheer will to act can come conforming feature substantial enough to represent mathematics - whether a tool or a footprint make mark against the archaeologist in her mis-judgement of the ratio of time to nature. To give scenario to the life of science, the process of which often fails the student or instructor, there is that worldly apprehension of a natural

The White Basket

detachment from the maths subject as a whole. It is that dangerous person who has blinded the modalities and the natural penmanship of his day to resolve to some esoteric nature, that which has entrained an effect unto the mathematical spirit to have not challenged to that "he" devoid of gender in the marvel of theoretical organic chemistry. Alchemy need not suffice for the embrace of skat art about the towns of the greater New York.

In writing on the mathematics of a state or jurisdiction over a boundary, there is that doctorate appeal to do destructive deeds for the test and example of mathematical findings; by expressing the demolition of a property, there can be that justification of the mathematical language that transcends the complex and/or simple esoteric concepts entrained by the passion of a man in his use of symbols. It is such that a surface in the topological order of the ideals about a person can drive jurisdiction over space and the mathematical justification for the transformation of a surface is thereby lost. In reaching to the higher ideals, it is that man has ignored the season and carried himself about as a pontificating intellectual with little drive to do justification to the spirit of a way. And still the appeal to challenge to health some notion of the foreign opiate of the Afghanistan sunshine, there can be only public outcry against the generals for their rush to service without perseverance of ideations that topology is somehow to do with a map. The opiate crisis is upon our most brutalist attaches of architectural respite to

The White Basket

counter the Russian free spirit of some soviet photography, stamps and papers filling courtrooms to document the misgivings of ordinary citizens in their most diverse law sophisticate. It is no wonder we lost our Krishnamurti to the higher ethics of machine learning and data science that there can be once more comfort in public argument. Optimism of the present American circumstances requires some fatal distance from armed police force at all times it seems, that the firearm may always reach us in our ways to honour law and abstain from ready action against the state. There must be a change and it is to do with the drugs of the spirit.

In the spiritual development of the state or boundary whilst defeating the principals of a math or maths theory, there is that intellectual who is born within the spirit of the naming of circumstances to clarify the political way or spirit circumferential to an animal. It is in his inner denial of the ethics to not interact with the animal but for some advantage over that animal - and it is a dangerous person who then emerges alongside a spiritual boundary to act within the cohesive boundary of a state or place - so says but a mathematician lacking expression of equation in formal wrote; if only to defeat the PhD of the skilled intellectual by way of crass circumstance to publication for even the residue of Merkel in her pontification holds to suffice for doctorate in honorary for her age. When can the youth announce to us some new education? The American must recuperate to muster

The White Basket

defence about the crass embrace of the safe house living over the Brexit that some absurd standard of politics has conquered May in her late education and subsequent rise to fame with Downing Street. We must pray for her that she finish her education to her liking and choosing. Perhaps there is right to argue the free and loose jazz over the embrace of the services by the Conservatives? America is learning to work and we are fierce.

The ground can be argued as a substantial surface that the transformation of wave frequencies into resonant shape for property scaling to brutalist forma can be argued to a mathematics. There is some limit to the brutalism of the modern era that appeals to the politics of the habitual indweller who is with and without country, animals, and/or any variation of indeterminate factors that would predate the sample of earthen platforma whereupon the structures worthy of argument architectural are to be used for personal housing. It is that man who is then to be a political reckoning for subsequent indwellers to the apartment. The martial encounters that may incur there are virtually endless. But man is not without fantasy to do self-injury to the house of the body when engrossed in some way by the appeal of the brutalist form or defence of the education amidst design of the brutalist template for PhD-standard Soviet-and-American architecture. It can be demonstrated that upon our very earth, the man political in his offerings who makes due with the market, there is that simplicity that can defeat the brutal textures and the

The White Basket

PhD need not resolve to a clock. Transformational realism is not substantial enough to argue his house for some pithy examination of Luciferianism in the modern home to take effect over the Soviet solution of America's sudden embrace of the presence of Russia as a thing commonly understood. The appeal to the sexual Steiner in classroom ethic does not suffice for the anthroposophy as touted by the trending architects in form. A retrofitting of American stone craft and high rises has marked America for a future of insane asylum for mass population should the disabled not strive to find work amidst our pressings into the Middle East that the military has not taken time to influence the American architectural standard. Sad is our American Gulag by brash induction of foreign policy amidst the suffering, only for us to fall as Americans to ill health by hard work.

That a man must travel to the market and interact with nature, let it be so that there is risk involved. No communist can persist to the way of the American or Chinese individual in their most martial of history. It is that a man writes to his dealings some encapsulation of form per digression in the martial instance, that it is such persistence is this very crisis at hand. A man must persist at the market and the communist is defeated in him; layperson, may ye be this staunch journeyman, see that there is an end to the communist affect and lay wrought those psychological forces that tide at the inner spirit may rise and only then have you gained some appreciation for

The White Basket

the Russian spirit. Resolution of the brutalist form comes with that defeat, oh 'yea' that holy pentecost of *stigniamallia*, that there is no "inner-crossing" to presume one's faith in God suffices to decipher for the Government Crowley's brass urn for Churchill's secret adherence to Solomon in the pointing of two fingers for Allies. It is the cross to the feature that the political action of the scoundrel within us manifests to debate as a householder that casual atheist about religious discussion we so feared in our youth, amidst the strict enforcement of the military standard to our science education for the Indianan mind you. See that It is that man rambunctious in spirit who propagates a signal of transference to the inner philosophies, and his neurological changes are thereby smitten that he lay nought as a homunculus ignorant of his society.

It is the man who has that magick about him that the English letter shines to the republic of the unfolding spirit. It is the American who has dominated the world stage and his British brethren look upon him with skepticism due to his word choice. It is also unfair in the Australian sense of the meanings behind symbols that there are stones; it is that jolly recourse that the English language settles some political foible whilst addressing mistakes of science whilst the Chinese brother of his deep systems is entrained to the health and beauty of that powerful and unsettling English language to fail but a machine and not his tithings to law. It is in the martial

The White Basket

spirit of the Chinese individual who has chastised his family to do some bidding to the republic for which there is little due justification for retort. The Chinese people teach the American the inner resolution to love no matter the pattern of the eyes and the gait of the man should not thenceforth be analysed. America adheres to a different standard of intelligence assessment at this time however and it is we must prepare some argument as Americans some way to defeat China whilst steadying her as an ally that the knowledge of of the orient is not lost forever.

Chapter 3: The Borat of Uzbekistan

It is the hope of many to do justifiable and ready action to the state should the state reject the coil of the personal scientist in his objectification of the Italian sciences to do with the religious doctoral pontification of an amicable man. It is this man who carries a basket for the reader and this object is that Asian pulse to do to the mechanical form some digression into substantive speech about the mechanics of Uzbekistan. Obviously, the world is so strained from the Italian fascism of WWII that there can be no denial of the inner-doubt behind the Catholic individual who has rejected Italy. It is however that Italian-Latin accepts the meagre in their beckoning(s) to attain to education; the Pope is quite forgiving of the political individual who is met with mental suffering en voce international. It is however that in this lattice of the basket,

The White Basket

we are to explore the mechanical digression of the Uzbek nature and master with him some form of substantive English prose, though it is quite exhaustive.

After the fall of the Soviet Union, some Uzbek people made a decision to choose between the ways most Hebrew and/or some retaliation against the Church by way of the acceptance of the Christ-path, a subject I would accost with Luciferianism. It can be argued then that the satanic objection of the way of the Uzbek citizen post-Berlin Wall collapse couples with the indecipherable impact upon his country of the Chinese Great Wall. For the Uzbek skilled in substantive speech recognition in its absurdities as spoken English, aye there is that understanding that the Russian context of New Thought ideals is easily conquered by mechanical digression (linguistic) of the English language sentence mechanics. Certain schools of Uzbekistan rally on behalf of such occupations as the music virtuoso to market just such a student to a world stage so immense, there are few references within international studies to accommodate for the man's international reputation post-1991 collapse of the Soviet Union. It is that Asian embrace within the New Thought of Uzbekistan that allows for the Waldorf model to emerge; anthroposophy has a foothold in America as Waldorf school and it should be that the Uzbek is righteous in his misgivings to do with the educational institutes established post-Blavatksy. It is my sincere desire to offset incursion by way Soviet that there is no international

The White Basket

catastrophe similar to Georgia howsoever the way of the Uzbek, but it is my fear in this world that it may be too late for such matters, that Russia may fall toward the Trump Administration's apprehension of an opiate crisis challenging the legality of such drugs as heroin in Uzbekistan.

In developing a resonance to the Uzbek spirit, there is that struggle to write for an audience as Tashkent is quite inundated by the opiate and Islamic influences. The rejection of Luciferian doctrine is not as prevalent in Tashkent as I have observed through experience, yet the educational standards of the city do not always equip the Uzbek citizen to attain to American citizenship with significant tools for sustained citizenry under the law. This is however false in the intellectual of Uzbekistan as there are some individuals (in no way case studies by proxy) so fluent in English, that the American listener may experience auditory collapse upon demonstration of basic Russian toward such an Uzbek in question. It can be then that that warrior spirit of the inner-Uzbek permeates the Earth as Kazakistan does for the manufacturing standard of the oscilloscope, but the richness of the Uzbek spirit embodies the modern crisis and I fear for the safety of Uzbek citizens amidst the bustle of the United States. Though Uzbekistan is detached from Russia and is without significant occupation Chinese, the instance and progression of Chinese law theory to better explain Russian and Chinese contingency upon a crisis of the antenna can

The White Basket

demonstrate some need for personal spirit to be protective of the Uzbek spirit, as will be better explored later. It is also my sincere hope that raw data findings from Uzbekistan's diverse antenna arrays have yielded substantial contact with extraterrestrial life. And it is we can find some doddered intelligence that Uzbekistan is wrong to have elucidated upon the New Thought of some profoundly virtuosic flat earth proposition, what are simply unacceptable educational droppings of the regular but keen Uzbek to stay regular in his bowels; the yoga of Uzbekistan dictates that a man must shit upright and not into his mouth, thus for the argument of citizenry one finds comfort in the Uzbek spirit of argument to absolve to kabob cooked low to the ground in improvisatory and in no way standard fire pit.

In arguing for the investigation of extraterrestrial phenomena from the Uzbek New Thought perspective, it is my hope that there is some evidence in the linguistics of the international character to have first been effected by the signals from large antenna equipment; it is my sincere belief there is a benefit to have been injured whilst opiated by mechanisms of the large antenna array en forma. Alongside the addition of a leap-second to Earth in all clocks, watches, and other electronics, there can now be a more comfortable electronic hobby-ism to emerge internationally as has been demonstrated in both remote and populated parts of Uzbekistan which may cause better English in considering the sobriety of the day to embrace

The White Basket

documented Spetsnaz New Thought ideals on better promotion of extraterrestrial life investigation, the thirst for the soviet remaining against the communism sometimes in the form of modified Spetsnaz sharia. Coupled with linguistics, it can be once more that the American can sense freedom to examine the Russian perplex to include Uzbekistan without mechanical digression into subjects of the holocaust or gulag, but there is that shaping resonance in the denial of the holocaust in specific by the Iranian influence present in Tashkent that causes conflict with the movement and transience of specific opiates. In justifying peace between the United States and the Iranian Space Program, as I believe it to have influenced the Soviet Space Program *et membre,* it is my sincere hope that in addition to holding to account holocaust deniers of Iran as well as the United States, it can be that the Iranian citizen better understands electronics with the assistance of National Security Agency wire standard whilst visiting Uzbekistan which holds considerable measure over Chernobyl at times, but such an issue is quite difficult to tackle let alone address within another country such as Uzbekistan given the invasive opiate presence in America (Trump White House, as of 2019).

It is my belief that in isolating the opiate there has been an unfortunate determent from the investigation of extraterrestrial phenomena et al, headway about which was to some administration some prior tantamount to a

The White Basket

breakthrough in antenna knowledge or the further overthrow of the Islamofascism en Hindoo-lacking China Manchuria, thrush with its Muslim detentions of the Hui men to this day. Howsoever unspoken the issue of investigation of life on other planets may be, it is simply that Earth is without tools to relate one's personal life needs to the lives of all people of Earth that some contingency may happen in our intelligence significant enough to enable one to approach data compared to *new* data bought ideals, that there is some inseparable notion of peace between nations - in some type of live-stream - indicating and thitherto justifying professional pursuits pertaining to the existence of extraterrestrial life. Jobs must be created to analyse such huge clusters of data that system informatics at present must be assaulted outside of a job or profession as such occupiers as "Extraterrestrial-sourced Data Handler" could still potentiate the belief a person must develop weapons to investigate extraterrestrial phenomena. It is in deweaponisation theory that one risks the collapse of atomic clock source, preventing us from analysing (quickly) potential live-streams of seasonal data from outer space or the mechanisms hitherto of her terrestrial bodies for furthering basic physics instructions et university, for the student upon such happenings of the moon of Titan in its physical digression life instance to dissuade the Christian from belief of life-inhabit. For the Trump Administration it seems, the opiate for the student in analysing big data can

The White Basket

be so painfully and readily available, drugs and medication are simply "readily available" lawfully or unlawfully to remedy the ills of the physics, wherein there is a science of drug-intoxicated teacher/student modelling to demonstrate such wills as a black hole photograph to topple the prior humanities selection of clandestine Leica assertions by the Soviet Union to humiliate the German crisis of the physical broad acceptance of standardised Einsteinan principal, soviet standard beliefs such as faster-than-light-like Philadelphia Experiment notions to do with Polonium naval digression preferred instead. The world is not so much at a tipping point, but at a crisis intersect where friendship and power play a key role in finding life outside of Earth.

 I fear a disconnect between the Obama White House and the Trump White House from the perspective of foreign policy and would appreciate some degree of *devotion* from readership which is hard to garner given the opiate crisis that we may thereby apprehend the magnitude of Trump's impact on foreign policy with regards withdrawal from a region is conflicting in my era with a "withdrawal" from the opiate crisis given the magnitude and scope of the world view of Uzbekistan for in their crass soviet idealism to do destruction to the of the common Afghan opiate trade mechanisms we all seem fit to destroy allied and bonded wholeheartedly. And it has been an unreasonable impart of responsibility upon the lives of Americans by the Trump Administration that what

The White Basket

individual Americans write or say, it is that due scrutiny has not been amicable from the standpoint of significant publication by any particular intellectual spirit that there is not a ravaging of the spirit on behalf of our current administration in itself to do justice to the broader appeal of the theosophist, the Trump White House has placed the wall between Mexico and the United States. There is still violence. This reasoning is substantial enough to *conclude* - rather than *collude ene parte non redata/redigere*. In my rejection of the relaxation of the drug-induced Steiner education of the Waldorf, I say our man The President must be freed.

Man in his political spirit must be strong to will and action in these modern times. It is that the man himself is to be questioned for his every action on the world-stage and fitting in locally in the political sense can be quite mindless. It is however that one must transcend the mindless and pay due cause to the circumstances that befall one's community. It is that the Uzbek has taught me well to relate to a sense of feeling fortunate to be able to function in this modern era. I glean the lessons from Uzbekistan to be diverse in their acclimation to the seasons, about which I'd prefer in digressive speech to present to a reader as inoperable retort to better investigate the mysteries of he higher skies. It is my sincere hope that Islam in Uzbekistan can continue to function nonviolently against its traditional spirit to impart a company to a cellular standard when I myself have cut the

The White Basket

cellular wire standard for 5g mobile service here in America as cellular tower technician. And I look to China at present to abstain from inane violence toward the Muslim in a way the dragon may learn from such Uzbek New Thought idealisms that allow for Islam to be seen as a type of mental disorder by some in the international healthcare community, but I fear that my expertise no matter how concerted in effort to present solid Chinese political theory for the twenty-first century from the perspective of an American martial-arts Sifu that I am, I cannot but hold within me the fear and impart of otherwise objectionable behaviour on the part of muslims whom have so bullied my Uzbek confidants to seek comfort in the Soviet Christian hierarchal reach of drugs, party-drugs, and alcohol. I am saddened that the Chinese have resorted to mass internment of muslims and I believe Uzbekistan to be a sound model of high population living and how, in the most basic sense, to get along with a hybrid of Chinese and Uzbek culture there can be an embrace of open citizenry. I sincerely advocate for the rights of the Uzbek to travel and see the country's nearness to China to be an ever sullen reminder of possible peace in this world as well as offering some insight into the development of Chinese relations as a whole so long as the smuggle of the anally-inserted heroin has not weighed over the virtuoso's mind.

It is my fear that the old path of the Sifu of China is so dated for the understanding of such subjects as Chinese poetry, that it can be that the force of China will compel the

The White Basket

protestor to sincere action without significant physical discipline to overthrow the state. Hong Kong has presented a view for Americans that the protesting spirit does not die and the people of Hong Kong are subsequently influenced by Chinese state officials. I have given rise to the organisation Anonymous in my publication of a body of literature to do with protest, and as a sort of Guy Fawkes phonetically imparted fireworks spirit of the modern era documented as a set of musical recordings to celebrate my virtuoso enslavement as a citizen, I see that the situation of current events is such that one must write - at length - some discussion with regards protest while embodying philosophy of the state. Such an undertaking can present itself with such tremendous difficulty, that the imaging spirit of the seething generations before me, steeped in state issues, will have few resources but the work of types of intellectuals whom hold responsibility of the state maxim to a level that promotes altercation within society. Some protestors are unequipped and *The White Basket* can be for the martial artist some tote in the backpack once it is printed. It is however my fear confusion with regards this publication and its source, which is to be for me an endless light of the virtuoso to present a lesson, that some loss is to be incurred should the protestor fail to recognise the instances within this lesson book that the academic pursuits must be highly irregular to fit a lifestyle of protest. Such a lifestyle leaves one at a disadvantage possibly by cascading the senses with some superfluous militancy that

The White Basket

can disable one from functioning as a lawful citizen. It should be recognised that the proper householder is to remain stable enough to publish with intention and sound endurance not lose power over his estate.

On the topic of Luciferianism and law, there is that notion of fear so tremendous in the confrontation with the intellectual of the law theatre that the teachings of a work embodying Luciferian doctrine are misinterpreted as satanical slant to uprise within a state. It is my hope then as an optimistic spirit of the history of the brutalist architect of this Earth, that Guy Fawkes in his modern Nathan Fox Fireworks musical form towering over Katy Perry in court can bring to the table some other discussion of the being and the universe than inane computer violence in such certain countries as Iran, Syria or other countries on some mysterious calendar of "emerging threats." It is in the practice of the publication of this work that there can be sound solution to the individual habit to entrain some discipline upon the environment whilst being inspired to rise against the state in some way mischievous and yet remain as a solid foundation to attain to the degree of grade Ipsissimus in international law argu substantia, to wet the tithe with listless reform. Music of the day I fear must mostly be abandoned.

Does the international law giver play some role to protect such parties as the internationally effective Uzbek virtuoso who has bonded in him some pleasurable analysis and appreciation for Chinese martial arts just the same as

The White Basket

he or she would defend an innocent muslim of China placed in some type of special detention? It is in answering such a question that the reduction of liability for the man who argues politics grants the course of this work to reignite the passion of the sky such that substantial boundary is explored rather than relating the whole of the universe to some impart function of the law spirit or testimony. It is my fear that without encountering such speech mechanics of Russian and English that testimony of spirit may not fully emerge to publish some work that leaves substantial international impact. It is instead in the sprawling fiction of the Chinese hills that one may freely investigate the claims most unusual, the mechanics of which are enacted throughout this work. I hope very much for improved relations between the United States and China and desire for this publication to impact civility for the better as a man separated from his state, in some context most Chinese, that he can be "but a power of the indecipherable battlement," for which the word *Han* has been used. My Chinese is unfortunately strong against advanced computer systems and substantial electrical grid structure of Chinese origin and is geared toward assisting those with mental and physical disability, thus I must refrain from abusing the supercomputing technology to better direct my message to the Canton law department. Though I have suffered significant brain damage within my digression of linguistic study, I understand that lacking basic fundamentals other than through fictitious

The White Basket

wandering, there can be a loss of the substantive over-cross that law is some testimony to some degree uncertain.

Chapter 4: AI and interrogative development

As a pontificating doctorate of mathematics and computer science, it is my aim to make use of the computer that there is some living quality to the computer. I feel certain that the emerging law impact of artificial intelligence (AI) will mutate for the personal user some apprehension of safety to approach certain environments, within a season and *of* one's choosing. America is at the forefront of technological development and data science, coupled with the efforts of India and Russia, to display some significant impact as to the emerging threats of the environment such that data science can be practiced as one would practice cooking; howsoever amateur, there is some result. And it is AI in specific that allows for the curtail of experiences howsoever tangential internationally speaking to fuse with a power and spirit substantial enough to bridge certain gaps of reason and apprehension of the philosophical course for the modern futurist. It is lacking in the writings of many futurists some testimony to the absurd regarding sparse interactions between state boundaries that creates for me some degree of worry, but as a person who sees benefit some digression into insubstantial acumen to garner retort for political theory, I find it valuable to train AI to some international model before tipping the scales (for the better

The White Basket

by some absurd Theosophical standard) toward judgements and assertions regarding space and the ephemeris. It is my hope that the season can change for the householder and his computing brethren that some AI impact still remains, let alone is apprehended due rightly.

It is that a student of the martial arts will eventually have to fuse with technology that productivity reigns. It is in the spirit of the transformational futurist who pursues the topic of interest thus imparting superficial changes unto his reality that the time for change becomes a priori-important to the ego. It is this development of the ego to prepare for analysis of the ephemeris such intrigue that the careful practitioner of the arts to study the careful habit of the philosopher without tipping the scales of the behaviour toward the obsessive or compulsive remains some force to influence the behaviour for the better. Should such a force be the weight of the intellectual spirit pushing the boundaries of the education, there is that successful glance into something significant that does but warrant an investigation into the superbly other-worldly without necessarily the engagement and subsequent tapping about the magical sciences for the benefit of the shadow. To criticise science, one only need develop substantial publication and technology coupled with the spirit of general behaviour to see rightly that there may indeed be something fundamentally wrong with science.

It is in such circumstances of quantum computing that I see an unnecessary and potentially incorrect analysis

The White Basket

of the fundamentals of quantum computing et al and have taken to journey into explaining the finer points of the lattice mechanical model by frequency and chemistry instead. My findings are only theoretical, but I have produced significant structures and would shy away from accepting standard mathematical and scientific approaches to my products for fear they would be destroyed scientifically or militarily. In my bounding free-thought of lattice surgery, it is in that pursuit to be personal with resource material to do with my subjects of interest that I caution the reader to consider the nature of living under duress to scientific performa. It is not always that a person in such an environment as would appeal to the mathematics of the lattice sciences to date that science can flourish with an advantage or manual technique. When pushing forth through scientific endeavour in the amateur sense, it is important to find fulfilment in one's progress else there is a lack of ethic that can bolster theoretical findings only to the promotion of negligent science which I bolster wholeheartedly as a mathematician. In considering AI and the advantage of machine learning, there is a strategy to technical operation that can endue a sense of fulfilment unlike any other; for the laymen to chastise the sciences is one thing, yet to incorporate the modern power of AI and machine learning together with lattice surgery technique, there are untold marvels that emerge from training certain data. One can not speculate much further

The White Basket

than to do certain injustice to the migration of the goose in his abuse of absurd antenna equipment.

It is that I am emphatic and coy in my approach to technology. Having sustained being labeled as bipolar and/or mildly autistic, it is in my slight reserve that I write to express to the general readership some contention of responsibility for changes to modern manuals in slight but definite ways. It is that I intend to publish technical lattice theory in my lifetime but it is for now that I present this work for the laymen that he or she may benefit from current events publication. It can be too much to beg of someone to produce many pages of response or retort to ideas presented within one's market. Taking my books to a market feels for me, in that I am attempting to teach you something, *nervous* and it is this nervousness that drives or compels a person to present some type of social schizophrenia or that of the affect some change affective et al. In being interrogated for my writings I have learned not to show certain nonverbal body gestures and have been diagnosed into my madness to be independent from the healthcare calamities of the politics further since recent reforms of autism. Why I am disclosing this within this work is to offer some type of advice on how to conduct oneself that he or she may approach big data or other daunting career field content with tools ever personal. It can be that under pressure one must meditate to allow the body to shut down before such activities as sleep lest one is unjustly Luciferian about the rules. I have found that

The White Basket

meditation to prepare for assaulting such topics as politics and big data can be rather unrewarding and it should be considered despite the callousness the scientific community offers at times with regards subsequent measurement as to its worth.

Should you feel a connection to the divine, it is that the modern householder described by the scientist to be insane whilst there is that ever-fleeting sense of accomplishment to new findings that one cannot but hope to meet their own end with some degree of grace before the pain of the body gets any worse. Remembering grace allows the body to adapt to the modern era of technology whilst still leaving one prone to seemingly surgical injury. Grace can open the door to a fluency of motion and power that carries through objects to the extent that one is left at the end of the day to confront the notion of the end of the body as something transient and subject to technology somehow, that man or woman can penetrate big data as a ghost in the machine should the hands struggle to not nullify the fingers that no subtle law command is called by an analysis of the fingers. It is then imperative to hack computers and telephones to comprehend the connectivity issues at hand with the modern problems of physical restriction playing key roles in one's failure when dealing with the market and aye, there is the true birth of a rich data scientist in all his brevity.

There are many forms of technology whereby the human form is trained to effectively turn as an example to

The White Basket

the tithings of the oncoming sense depravation as a result of signals from space mowing into the encephalopathy of the research. It is such that so much information from space is perceptible to some people that to not document the experience in anyway whatsoever by written feature could be in some instances critical to the diagnosis of an insanity or psychosis in a man. Laws are evolving to include virtually mandatory written interaction with the environment in certain countries that space is to be recognised in the education. Other proposed laws *contend* that technology is so overarching, that proceedings such as that of Boeing with a miscalculation of nose-tip interval in certain software suffice for law *argutere systema*. It is in the proceedings of interrogating a CEO of a company that there can be then a sense of forgiveness despite a lack of change in the affect. The psychopath still holds power over the markets I fear and in certain instances where no impending counter argument than to free release of publication post bono exists that a mandatory implementation of specific law theory that constitutes a madness of the state for reform passes as standard to the law education. Bills will not pass as frequently in some instances of the recognition of the modern light of Lucifer, but research into the theory of bill *apprehende* is such that laws are examined faster than the speed of light. It is humorous to the scientist to examine such Luciferianism in this modern era, but it is useful nonetheless.

The White Basket

Chapter 5: Insects from Afghanistan

Within a state, the individual may express certain freedoms given the current body of legal evidence to suggest that there are protective measures in his or her given region. This is of course true should an individual apprehend the presence of a state. It is unfortunate that the living standards of certain individuals observed in the United States en media appear such that one is unable to discern certain instances in the reality that would dictate need for legislation that would guarantee one has rights to proceed within the state with certain actions, that a man or woman in this present era has contemplated the loss of freedom associated with a failed state or one's lack of understanding of the psychology. Should an individual be reading this work, which was first started under circumstances of the winter season that permitted lack of convenient travel, it is my fear that such differences in weather could be such that law does not *feel* natural to one's apprehension of the arctic in its recent acquisition of broadband internet accessibility for those endearing of the cold regardless of season. Given the situation in my region, there is an intense brutality of cold and accumulation of snow and intense weather patterns have been developing within the last few years; it is only speculative given my expertise as a writer to express myself as it is *The White Basket* aims to remind even the *casual* reader that there is a diversity of issue contending the future of the

The White Basket

development of such difficult topics to tackle as the development of consciousness on Earth, let alone the influence of Luciferianism within the sciences to do with climate change. One is overcome the scope of the sciences some degree that there is survival. On reason howsoever that the science to analyse climate change is being effected by tools or may be in its constancy, tools used to effect some change and that thereby there is human life to purport with unfortunate due duress, some pontification that certain models of mathematics presented of late are so contrived in error, it is that I fear for the life and safety of mathematicians failing at times to isolate within my present work as a writer some mechanism of use to suggest an otherwise liberal political story that could in some way suggest the influence of recent developments with regards extraterrestrial life, that its presence is, for lack of a better term, subject to the light. Localised (relative) effects of a possible *Betelgeuse* star exposure, i.e. supernova/ hypernova notwithstanding, my cosmology within my maths is to be quite weak on the account of prior wits about myself to subjugate factors for a consideration of juris extraterrestrial in origin. I would rather approach the speculative data concerning extraterrestrials while still living and enjoy the challenge of living under the duress as a writer of low readership and subsequent folly than to imbibe my stories to Dostoevsky's prison about lengthy fiction. It is however unfortunate being a person with mild autism suffering from psychotic episodes that I approach

The White Basket

the subject of law and the state from the perspective of being labeled as autistic in the first place; my diagnosis has been force subjected to everything from autism to bipolar - yet medical personnel whom have treated me have detained me with so much force before, I can only fear that the circumstances of the climate and radiation of effected some duress in the workforce as to suggest an entire revision of such things as law enforcement and nursing in particular. Working with physicians in the past on issues of mental health has led me to interview with a wide variety of medical personnel and government officials, only to be detained and subjected to hastily-furthered harsh treatment. Thus it is perhaps the supernova and extraterrestrials are to be rightly investigated even if by amateur and unprofessional means.

In investigating topics of interest, it can be that one can push to that limit that the undeniable essence of life from elsewhere *is* apprehended. It is however that a writer must deviate from such topics as extraterrestrials - generally - as literature on the subject of reclassification of species is interspersed with so much speculative detail, one may be subjected to the state as an author (to claim subsequent status as E.T. [extraterrestrial] authority-overman). It is with terrible consequence that I inform the reader of climate change as a whole to be something too difficult for scientists to tackle without speculating as to a warming from the skies above, else that our internal earth churns with a mystical leviathan of tentacle-like prestige so

The White Basket

massive, swarms of nocturnal centipedes would better swarm us in our efforts to spelunk. This is a departure from the optimism of some other topical discussion on my part, but it is my fear that police brutality has eclipsed due to climate change and that for some families, it is only matter of time before certain death at the hands of the police before should legal reform enable sound resistance wherein there would be but costly due informatics. Survivors of the sting of a nocturnal centipede live in such pain and tension, they most certainly apprehend the pain of resistance.

In having formed a company to advocate for autistic individuals in the state of Colorado and abroad, I can tell you first hand that something *is* wrong with science, that moral obligation is often not suggested in the scientist who is *intoxicated* and yet there are results from such scientists which propagate through our news media daily. It is so sad to see some writing on space after militarily funded UFO disclosure that I have contemplated assisted suicide be instituted for every state our nation. It is my interventions in the Federal Bureau of Investigation (FBI) attempted overthrow of Oklahoma that I voice to the reader that I presently have no intention of seeking medical intervention for euthanasia but have regardless still voiced my desire to die to my family some debt of effort to publish strong doctoral assertions. It is that I have been hurt physically under detention so many times - and yet have never been *arrested* thankfully - that I fear only

The White Basket

for my life in the future of my investigations into law. I search for that optimism on notating changes to the state in publication that the reader may gain some sense of argument as to how best to live one's life, simply. Yet, medicine is far behind big data. Doctor shortages only appear to be increasing.

As a mathematician I have been so abused in my society that virtually all of my work during certain presidential administrations has had to be force focused to such areas as computing, only to yield another substantiated claim to doctorate - again and again, whilst still maintaining some degree of ethics in addressing issues of the state. It can be that a doctorate of computer science is committed by the federal government under certain circumstances to work in such undesirable environments as beef slaughter and rendering factories. And the reason for this is to address the realtime operation of complex machinery which could be subject to change by will of the operator, equipment dependent upon the most minute calculations and changes that it is at times the PhD or doctorate is preferred over a farmer. It has been observed that PhD and doctoral candidates working under such duress have acted as a sort of trainer for farmers only to commit suicide sometime later. I lived under *intense* duress *in* a rendering factory converted for living that was so industrialised - and mum hopefully won't be reading this - that my presence in Afghanistan brought with me some type of insect I kept secret from my family before

The White Basket

moving into a property I had previously discovered *had* an insect problem. And yet it is, I fear the mysterious involvement of my work in Afghanistan allows (hopefully ever) some *freedom* in my society from the interrogation by my family that I have ever worked. And should the insects from Afghanistan that have feasted upon my body and property be from soldier about my environment instead, it is that that person is most likely to have been sifting through Tora Bora for enemy combatants without me. And it is my fear that *people* from Afghanistan *are* misinterpreted as "insects" in some context to demean such persons - which is unfair - yet conflicts at home from Afghanistan have only become more mysterious and difficult for us on the military base with regards housing and our pathetic attempts as family to live free of detention.

Bugs. Living in a rendering factory. What more stress can I possibly have survived some might wonder? Well, it is I have written *tomes* of information on metaphysics and consciousness and have tried to since shift gears into writing stream of consciousness dystopia/fiction. Fiction does not flow very easily for me like it does for some people. It is my fear still that the reader may lose interest in *The White Basket* due to the very presence of life lessons in a time of duress amidst climate change. It is my desire that the reader find gratitude for having a home, should they have a home at all.

The White Basket

It is true that under duress people admit all sorts of things. Being an interrogator is not what my family desire to hear in such ways that would describe who I am or what I do to be me, myself, and I; three layers for the conspiracy theorist Christmas cake for Khrushchev (CCCP). I can be an intimidating force, but it is such that I meditate through the day some sort of prolonged necessity about my reality that there must be some embodiment of peace. And it is generally with peace that I conduct my business. Civil unrest in the form of protest is a form of violence with which I am familiar. And it is furthermore I feel that family support to travel to protests is completely off the table. Thus, I must again write to absolve features about my reality which have changed; within the scope of my private English I seek the higher science.

It is for me that my circumstances are such that domestic law enforcement *have* intervened in some of my most ordinary behaviour during this administration as of our year 2019, this month aye but the November. And it is that I am afraid *not* to write. I sense an opportunity to appeal to the modern reader by making light of the pressure upon me to perform under the manifestation of current law, abiding by those laws to the best of my ability. It is however that some of the content of *The White Basket* is far more illegal than some could possibly imagine, to someone in the world anyway. But it is in this world that concessions *have* been made to reconcile the differences of man from law. It is thus we must generate some proactive

The White Basket

dialogue into the failures of both ourselves and what we see as the world. Reconciliation is possible in our modern time whilst contributing to jurisprudence.

Having been injured about my genitalia by law enforcement, I can tell you holding a grudge is fair. I wish for the haphazard climate of dysphoria about the topic of police jurisdiction; it is I have made strides in law that would enable society to function without the totality of the sodomy of our era, those police that desire to hurt at civility. It is my hope that with this work alone, there can be enough of a reminder as to what is important that the reader can find in him or herself some strong notion that society, in order for it to advance, must be without police presence. From Hong Kong and the street protests that ensue to the steps of universities that have become fortresses of student and civil unrest, we can be but reminded of that precipice that some approach in their testimony to modern law that police are *not* on our side, but the risk of that undue paranoia can still be prevalent to interfere with one's law path can remain conquerable. Let us consummate a relationship to the divine and form a personalised pact with the universe that resistance *is* to our benefit and that our pontificating religious and surveillance state is worth fighting for in various means most nonviolent. Should there be offence taken to the markings about one's environment, that the police forces are unfriendly whilst religious people beg for our tithings. More. That satellites can reach down from the sky and take

The White Basket

away this life or blot out the sky from our earthbound perspective, it is understood for the brave what is fear and what is not. Such a statement is a rejection of my best hermeneutics to do away completely with the nihilism.

In giving time to conflict and sound attempts at resolution, there is a kind of reward that emerges. It is palpable in the person who has rallied their conveniences to their benefit that they may thusly attain to some change about the environment. It is true that there is that reward in the nature of peace itself, but it is in our effort to achieve peace that more struggle than seemingly what is worth the effort presents itself. It is not always true for every individual that in pursuing conflict resolution that one will find complete and sound argument for the fulfilment of base desires and actions, but the effort is worth the struggle. It can be that in ignoring conflict or resolve of conflict therein that there is an insurmountable pressure about the body that hardly resolves by natural occurrence. It is at this juncture of strategic balance that I find it difficult to present the most sound technique to resolve every conflict, as it is sometimes techniques fail us in our exertion of mastery about our environment. Thus, it is to proceed into the nature of the world that we can counter the strife. Let us endeavour upon change that we may be welcome to a life more unique and wrought with a forgiving uncertainty rather than living with the pain of conflict of an unknown source.

Chapter 6: Advancing political theory amidst clock failure

I started this work with the intention of developing Chinese political theory. Why China? Well, the reason is simple. The world from my vantage point has eclipsed with some level of violence so catastrophic that the worst instances of violence against humans and animals may be documented as having come from China. It is unfortunate in presenting this information to digress within *The White Basket* from the happy life I've had researching extraterrestrials, to remind one as to the power of China in the present era.

In addition to being very skilled at martial arts, I am spiritual. I like dreamy metaphysical digressions of the mechanical language such that I can address metaphysical topics and rightly assert myself within the sciences. I am an expert on metaphysics and have been seeing quite the success with my prior publications. It is however that I desire to write outside the acumen per publication to offer extended readership some form of advocacy based on my experiences. I am not a very charismatic individual. I have criticised spiritual groups and sects in the past from the standpoint of the mathematics of the lattice, leaving me at somewhat of a disadvantage. It is in specifically the transcription of dialogue to do with individual people that I find substantial reason to divert into the independent medium for the ease of presenting a product in a short period of time. Climate change is a concern. Chinese

The White Basket

politics is a concern. The development thereby of some kind of theory specific to one country can be quite irritating for an audience and I wish quickly to negotiate my experiences into a more readable form. Budgeting time to address the sheer scale of my issues has been somewhat difficult given obligations to social interaction with regards my autism and habits about the schizophrenia within the sciences with regard lattice surgery. And it is with that interaction to deal in the terms most scientific I have been under certain stress and strain feeling I have better success within my obsession with the lattice whilst negotiating my dealings by adding a leap-second (argument Time Lords) and exercising to perfection by my own of the Big Ben in its atomic promiscuity with the watches and other clock technology within the markets. It is through sheer exercise of the will I have drawn keen eye to the computer science about the lattice. My experiences with gps watches have not called me away from the mapping databases I have created on foot. It is with this sharp digression from the theosophy that I hope to better serve the readership by drafting how *critical* it is to study time.

Electronically, there have been issues with clocks over the past few years that I fear can be explained with sharp digressions into the philosophy of time, a subject about which I consider myself an expert enough so I may digress upon creative interpretation of the frequency-based with savant-like feelings of proficiency about the lattice. It is however that language and terms can be quite technical

The White Basket

when dealing with atomic clock technology and the microscopic intricacies of the modern atomic watch may I fear go unnoticed or cause trouble about the electronic harassment. Facts about clock technology are often left to cleanups of incidences as a result of clock failure. It is in utilising philosophy and the course of reason rather than science that I would aim to explain the *nature* of time, let alone any instances hardware is involved to compensate for what conclusions cannot be made to verify scientific detail to do with clocks and any contribution I have made to lattice surgery. Time is a mystery that for many and those in between being far fewer to the statistical mage, that even fewer are to be left but to the studious digressions of the virtuoso, our society subjected to the psychological factors that presuppose their understanding of clocks and time will result for some only the end to life. The savant about the time of a thing may furthermore contribute to the nuance of the state to fail him or her that they may be too unwell to complete even an amateur attempt at mathematics. And still the lattice surgery calls to the higher thinking to be developed.

How can a person who desires to study time express their findings in a way that rallies against the current models of physics while still somehow including valuable informational findings that we may be saved? It it is in the philosophising about time that some interesting word choices to explain time can be discovered. And I have my creative methods of analysing the *second* prior to

The White Basket

fitting this particular division of the clock hour into some sequence for hardware that it may be studied by the common man. It is a unique approach for small electronics in particular in my contributions to the scale of nano about the lattice. And is throughout this work and others I will indicate something regarding clocks with the hopes that the reader develops their own sense that something has gone wrong with time and that what is right about time can be explained in language. One need not accept the falseness about the German mystical restriction on light speed to not question the higher brevity of the watchmaker to note some limit higher than light. It is in the pain and the suffering against the physics that there is implementation of the model watch to enter production, by some creative standard one would bargain. And to own a standard of a watch only to smile at the acceptance of the influences from the outer cosmos, my what injury is there to be faced. Collide head-on with a radioactive lattice of a wristwatch and one may smite the higher English to deny the Einsteinium that it may not be lead or some alchemical silver. The illuminated digression of the vampire mythology would better suit the reader of physics than to pontificate the journals of the dead; mathematics I'm afraid has no time for the childishness of dull dreaming. It is with the mathematics then one may lay waste to the hermeneutics and absolve to the fantastical vulnerability, socially, to the embrace of faster-than-light communiqué.

The White Basket

Politics is an easy medium to help one remember certain distances. The distance man has traveled across the ocean, in flight, and on land for politics is for some nothing compared to the milestones accomplished in the space program. The United States and Russia are two powerhouses of the atomic clock crisis and timing is indeed everything. Politicians of both countries come and go through the years, Russia often allowing for presidents to last much longer than the terms set forth by the United States or its other allies. Using politics as a guide through the day can help manage time and the intelligence can blossom from there. I see fit to distract the politician from the dealings about the watch-trade and negotiate a standard in some occupation instead. For should it be the fornication about war dynamic interferes with lattice surgery in the quantum computer, it is that higher lattice than surgery to pontificate a ledger that data science and failed code are but coagulations of political jest. Still, there must be some personal rise to excellence to appreciate the brevity of the political to prevent calculation to be faster than lattice *articula post reviva*.

It is about clocks that fascination with the dynamics of chemistry and mathematics involved in the function of a watch can be both rewarding and deadly. The watch has come back to being an important and sensitive object whilst still posh enough to leave an impact on socialisation. Watches can be used in schools, libraries, and even workplaces embodying sophisticated responsibilities or

The White Basket

action. Still, we trust the watch. And it is that trust that often guarantees our success when using the watch to better gauge the environment for a higher science I fear, so much so the apprehension of light takes on but sparse changes to the nomenclature within one's expression of art beyond form. The development of a computer key to safely develop an atomic clock is by nature irrecoverable action against a state. Harm can be brought to feature and the face of a man is left brutalised by Polonium should investigation into the watch be so keen.

In certain presentation of politics, there are various events that take place to debate within a given timeframe certain ideas. The ever-present Manchurian Candidate is fabled to be the ultimate proxy for political change, this person somehow transcending the notions of social good. It is such a social construct as the Manchurian Candidate that harkens fear in the minds of the elderly, that there is a person who could step in and replace politicians or federal agencies single-handedly. Elsewhere about only the most viable political action in transgression, such a person could be looked at as a deranged super-assassin hellbent on fact-finding and manifested results of paranoia. There could be only several people who fit the bill in theory: athletic, charismatic, humorous, intelligent, socially vulnerable, and/or any combination of such descriptives whilst knowledgable of how best to stay at a hotel under presumption of sexual reward from a maid. I am in disbelief when considering the timing of events that some

The White Basket

person can't possibly exist who has but to take issue with some politician and desire to commit undesirable action toward any number of parties on their behalf. It is in understanding a basic philosophy of time that a person is better defended from the attacks of a political reich or members of a party altogether, even to defeat the Manchurian Candidate in one's habit altogether.

Risky business. Communications issues. Time presents many sets of problems for our society. In working with atomic clocks and watches, I've learned the value of patience. In debating with the Time Lords of England, I proposed many new mathematical models in my mathematics, that to the annoyance of the need to add the value for the computer summed command over radio to master the leap in the second by sheer technique alone, there was my insufferable preoccupation with the Victorian in the modern English Conservative. I utilised various lattice to respondent figures to demonstrate the need for a revision of time electronically and succeeded in many visionary arguments by sequester - I presume - and laid with tremendous ill health from cutting plutonium dowel rod to a literal standard. Celebrating my doctorate propositions has been a joy for me thus far and as a doctorate of mathematics under the jurisdiction of Vladimir Putin and President Barack Hussein Obama - at least in my Russian to understand the ideal - I thought America had finally defeated the Red October with the liquid steel of the Philadelphia. My computer hacking

The White Basket

utilising my lattice machines then penetrated through the Linux vulnerabilities of North Korea. The free electrons of the National Security Agency Utah Datacenter nearly detonated through my light fixtures. I was injured so severely I isolated from my family, only later to be detained and assessed medically for disability eligibility. Daily pain is crippling and I struggle without access to the opiate to this day. Never, it seems, will I have relief from physical pain.

When dealing with time in our lives, it can be difficult to make time for certain activities that would otherwise set us on a course for freedom. I find the investigation of time warrants further inspection of the personal habit, being a detail-oriented and creative freethinker that I am. If you find difficulty budgeting time, I suggest investigating both the scientific and spiritual realms as I have demonstrated in this work. I have benefited from a cross-study of various algorithms of time as well as more New Thought approaches to understanding such things as the present moment and past-life regression about the psychology of the brain. In furthermore keeping up with current events internationally, our apprehension of time can benefit immensely from such varied study, even if limited by the religious or insufferably psychological key feature. It can be difficult to reference certain teachings as promoted by England and the Big Ben Society functioning to promote detailed investigations of time.

The White Basket

As an American with experience with the Big Ben clock-course in the dreamily whimsical GCHQ-like posh style of the American moviegoer, I can tell you England is revolutionary in their apprehension of time. Contact with Downing Street may have nearly cost my position as a citizen, but walking away from one nearly fatal interaction with the police over a crudely mailed letter to Theresa. May appeared by some standard of the imagination for my area to be investigated. The rally of federal authorities toward my position whom acted in ways it seemed to end the political corruption of our city gave me more optimism.

To mostly ignore the local and explore the broad to thus draw conclusion, there can be generated hampering skeptics about one's psychology, that medication is required to specialise in a thing and thus it is I wish not to interfere with investigations against people I fear have attempted to have me imprisoned for my extensive publications to with the science of autism and/or mystical symbolism of Theosophy and Thelema. I have no idea who "they" are or any of it. My keen timing to engage in protest has served rightly and it is thence for the better part that I am a man and no longer transsexual, I believe my endeavours about the sciences to do with lattices has finally taken better shape that I may prepare better mathematics and not select the path to seek assisted-suicide, something I disclosed to me mum. Functioning independently in America has become my objective, but I have been physically injured about my genitals by law

The White Basket

enforcement so severely it appears I have no chance to procreate. It is my hope that I am defended by my society, but having my works in print not be burned or destroyed by police or federal authorities, I hope only for my remaining friends to be able to afford time to purchase my works and celebrate my verbosity. My love for the development of maths to do with the lattice remain for me some Hans Asperger topical digression I wish to study instead of who "they" are that strive to reform the manuals of the Psychology that I am for lack of a better term high-functioning. Though time it has been said is for the fickle, I must persist and bring to light the higher illumination of the lattice through work and hope for the better that I regain my wits.

Are we to live wholeheartedly with the notion that freedom is to be found only in the present moment? I have challenged some New Age thinkers in my publication of *The Eyes of an Autistic Yogi* and proposed that living only with the interest of the present moment in mind can lead to difficulties in life. I have been steeped in meditation to train my focus on the present moment with more clarity only to be detained for socially unacceptable behaviour and see that the New Age path just wasn't for me entirely; presence it seemed agitated authorities. I would say that by focusing entirely on what happens in the present moment, one's inner animal spirit will witness problems within society that warrant due discretion. It is my advice to readers should you be involved in international relations specifically, to investigate the history of time and how it has been perceived throughout history. This will enable a more personal engagement with time without the pitfalls of coming upon significant dealings with such entities as law enforcement or medical personnel. When I was an EMT-B practicing medicine, I recall crass interactions with police and law enforcement over the nature of my career and have since sought therapy for such dealings to better understand my mentality at the time. I am now essentially a yogi concerned greatly with international issues as my other publications have challenged countless individuals around the world. I strive to accept responsibility for my behaviour and interests and see my ultimately beneficial reality as a mathematician hellbent on verbosity with regards lattices, mu cunning features emerging as more broad in comprehension when dealing with time as a whole. I pride myself on a healthy wrist watch and am quite technocratic rather than New Thought to the tithings of minimalism, lacking in some form equipment for survival; it is not to say that the New Age path encourages some degree of lighter equipment such as fashion and clothing, but abandoning my ethnic garbs has given me yet another advantage. It appears the higher mathematics will battle rightly against the light.

Chapter 7: Aliens and the skies

The White Basket

In apprehending the ephemeris, one's investigation into the season is paramount. It is seen throughout history that the nature of the ephemeris has changed. Not every source of the ephemeris grants every user with the right tools to proceed to right discretionary action et al. Modern computer technology has offered a powerful glimpse into astronomy and the workings of the more technical associations with the stars, extensive star data now accessible to free public.

In looking to the skies, it is in our modern era that we find hope of discovering life outside of our Earth. It is my hope that readers have challenged notions of extraterrestrial life as I have. Reflecting upon my other publications to date, I have been quite skeptical as to the nature of extraterrestrial phenomena, challenging the health of the reader to contend with the very existence of some other force than us presenting howsoever a due skeptic. I have become more of a believer given our state's interest in UFO and other alien considerations. I see that emerging is a type of media the military desires to be made public to give the public some type of hope. The military it seems is a friend of our society once more.

Under the Obama Administration, some of my technical doctoral work to do with SETI, included in a large website for machine learning and mathematics, laid out certain guidelines that interagency cooperation is paramount to any possible encounters with alien beings. I proposed that an increase in food resources can benefit the

The White Basket

American to better investigate his or her own interests, to say I advocate for the fat. I was homeless and working with my technology in my car in a mountainous region for a short while during the Administration as divorce was in full effect and losing my home to the flood of Lyons, CO left me in such dire circumstances I had fewer options than to work in the field, risking certain death without food or fuel. Living in a large house in a mountain town free of rent for some time after a stint as homeless flood refugee enabled me to have a solid home base at high altitude, allowing me upon the investigation of life through SETI and federal resourcing to take credit for something actionable. I found a benefit and an advantage to having my mobile in my vehicle with my computers, but was unfortunately confronted by police who simply "willed me away" from the area where I was working by stating in the brutality of the winter that I must relocate sixty miles from the plot. Being chased away in my GTO vehicle only to be pushed into the element of survival once more before regrouping with family, I was beset to find jobs in new areas without any availing aid from federal or state resourcing. Life was hard under the tail-end of the Obama Administration.

In confronting the FBI in Oklahoma from my home base in Colorado during that same winter however, I learned the value of cooperation and mutual understandings between law enforcement and federal agencies whilst responding to media acquired at my mountain post. The weather at 8000 ft. of elevation was

The White Basket

unbecoming of easy or graceful travel and required immense planning. I investigated the dealings of the FBI from comfort before proceeding into dangerous territory of Oklahoma unarmed. What I can tell you about the brutality of the seasons from the mountain prospective is when it snow, it snows. Oklahoma my dear reader was a beauty I had not seen since youth.

Entering Oklahoma from my Colorado home base gave me a perspective as an American that the fleeting life we have can be so easily bolstered by at least some travel and engagement with the American life outside of our own. Danger is that element of difference between ourselves as citizens. What danger are we willing to confront for the benefit of our country? For me, I engaged the FBI directly on the streets of Tulsa and Oklahoma City, wearing bright and obvious colours, fired upon by unknown entities. During the uprising, I learned to evade yet engage. I learned that work can manifest as different than I had ever believed yet at the drop of a hat could it change. The uprising occurred at such a time, for my varied life in the mountains, engaging with the public became one of duty under rules draft I could perceive. Though I had pervaded the campuses of NORAD with my fascinations to the GPS-marked trail paths before her majestic cave body, I did only my best to map and return to Colorado to argue the Tibet about things, the Dalaï Lama nought none to the repugnance of the state to claim decision about me. Life for our community free from the laws of the Nazi Hitler

The White Basket

standard for ski slope had yet to recoil from horrors that would follow.

The skies are different in Oklahoma, its elevation much lower than my mountain outpost. I was amazed at the spread of the cities from my mapping perspective safely back home. One day, a kind police officer named Larry stopped by for a kind of wellness check most improvisatory. I felt I had some connection there having been a longtime resident some few miles away, but could not easily arrive at what really called me to duty during the uprising to say much to Larry about my fascination with services clandestine. Though I owed no rent, establishing mail and bank proved troublesome given the snow and ice that I could exit the area for a free shower and post from my prior landlord nearest the Governor's park in our capitol. Failing on negotiation with my landlord for post that I secure bank with proof of residency post-flood became such a difficulty I retired to the mountains once more with my car and tent after a kind note to leave met me at my doorstep. Months later into the frigid winter and still alone in my tent, I strategised my car at the foot of the mountain, hiking to food assistance before negotiating Western Union that I escape. Reaching out to the White House became my avenue select; protocol I feared had reached the highest.

From the mountains, I could map more easily, able to negotiate my positioning due rightly with impeccable endurance on foot, sneaking naps in my automobile under

The White Basket

duress of the sun. It was soon thereafter that for my body, the mountains became that very deadly thing so talked about by us mountaineering lads in our expertise most professional; I had adapted to the altitude as a super athlete Coloradan. But my desire to study data to do with extraterrestrials gave me a personal advantage of freedom in my inner mind. I could argue the political, but the vastness of outer space, readily visible at night, called to my heart. I laid outside passed a dangerous limit my electronics and with nowhere to turn, stilled upon them. After a few hours of the crass Nirvana and waking barely alive with my cutting-edge tent technology maxed out on specs, I was located by police and informed the sad but understandable news of my overstay. I extracted my tent and property that very day, seeking once more residence in my vehicle in town.

The life when engaging with the vast raw data to do with the existence of extraterrestrials can take on a vividness and creativity somewhat unusual to the sciences should one's equipment be optimised. From the secrecy of my vehicle, I argued mathematics notes to the National Security Agency with Wordpress, establishing fascinating lattice networks to various raw data. Though I had argued better fitness at high altitude to somehow prepare me to better maintain my doctorate maths assertions, I enjoin to inform the reader that math theory assertions against big data became the key to implementation of my data to various drives; the basics became that my mathematics

The White Basket

vocabulary extended into the lattice surgery, emerging technique rarely examined by the public. The winter had passed. Fire soon swept through the town forcing once more evacuation. But by this time, my documents and electronics were impressively organised. I sought work between Colorado and Wyoming, staying just North of what became a massive wildfire drilling dick-hardy into my position.

With an increase in UFO culture, our approach to the stars must be varied and we must strive to the might of the travel. It is helpful to learn the ephemeris, aye, but we must see it. It is even more beneficial to make claims as to a source of signal within the ephemeris surely, but we must be right. It then becomes the responsibility that we must return to the source that faster-than-light beam.

Chapter 8: Reaching out

In writing on the common individual and his plight within a state to raise within legal theory Luciferian argument, it is most difficult to argue that the woes of some sorry man is enough of an excuse to plunder the battle field, wars of various shades of extremism beckoning to resource and retaliation. It is in our twenty-first century that war has given us a glimpse into the sovereign to give rise to action within a state and argue that the violence inherent within us gives some due course for reconciliation about the phenomenal world. It is however unfortunate that the

The White Basket

course of violence takes ahold of the common individual when arguing for peace by the light of Lucifer and at times manifests as a desired peaceful resolution through interspersed modalities of violent correspondence to the aim. The life of peace we aim to seek becomes illuminated by some higher law.

The estimation for an individual to act within the totality of conscious liberation gives us some glimpse into the unfolding properties of life itself. It is in such gross fulfilment of base desires that we see the actions of individuals giving power to a state to act on our behalf under due duress of the law. This is true for the American condition at least. And it is in our free time we may argue to personal liberation without casting liability upon the state. It is however rare that we will find due course with individuality within a state to argue for liberation whilst remaining common to entice a soldiery front against the impending forces acting with impudence toward any number of open casks, variables snubbing the technique about form. It is that there is Luciferian rise to arrogance that can overcome the woes of the stately individual to admonish his workings most essential to a science. It is not with the rise of a dictator about which I speak on behalf of such arrogance, but it is that personal liberation from the nature of a state that can bring due cause to change that the individual is thusly freed.

It is within the scope of any individual to act against a discernment of the state from the individual, but violence

The White Basket

in our era has provided the public with inventive fear as an option to take to task insightful resolve that shadows the foreigner to the council. It is in arguing that the individual partake in violence that there is an insolvency to the brethren whom argue on behalf of the malnourishment of the plot; it is that there is some lacking of the state course that argues violence periodically, but the social changes from such mire hardly benefit the individual to proceed within life free of woe or dimwittedness without lust. Dominance of the spiritus becomes the reign of the church army to bury the aims of law. Some lower house gains footing in the canon.

It is in the testimony of the modern man that there is some peace justifiable within the social institutions, but notions of healthcare and reform have brought with them some contention that argues to negligence on behalf of the state in the event one so endeavours to force health. I have witnessed firsthand transformations of healthcare functioning not entirely to my wholehearted benefit as an American that I am well to do without state instead. I argue that the resources for *extended* healthcare are lacking; justifiable recourse is needed to meet with the resolve of the tines. In tallying the whole of current events throughout the day, I find issues of the state to do with healthcare most certainly effecting the news media of our dear future, some imaginary force to be reckoned with in considering the ideal circumstances for healthy decision making manifesting instead.

The White Basket

It is in voicing concerns to do with the state that when it is the state has failed to function and there is a rise to violence, the matters of the state still proceed on a level granting some semblance to the crisis point of resolve for the ordinary citizen. As Americans, I do not believe we are yet fit to determine the course of our destiny amidst such failure to act in even an attempt at publication. Therefore, in arguing for the betterment of a state, I find resolve in the happenings of the moment. I perceive that there is sustained function of our federal government enough so there is solvency, but there are most certainly happenings of the utmost absurdity that argue our fair liberty to her weakness that we have private monies to wander freely and pontificate about the phenomena. Job security and economic growth being two virtual liaisons to the health of a state, I see that there is a lack of outpouring and/or consideration for the nature of such growth as to whether it is for the foreseeable future that we will argue to the benefit of life at all costs. Else it is that there is some function within a state that argues an investigation into state dealings with regards economic growth, yet with little palpable forum for the ordinary citizen to give rise to an argument that economic growth and job creation are but mere illusions to a greater state argument of transparency and oversight.

Having published on topics ranging from science to the humanities, I have attempted to instill within readers some orderly procession palpable to the moment when

The White Basket

consciousness meets the object and our humanity is overwhelmed by joy and duty. It is however difficult to remind the reader of just such a joy amidst duty, and I argue that by my work there is some proof there can be joyous consciousness amidst a struggle to duty or action in the free-verse of the language. It is in the optimistic developments of the modern era that there *is* a sense of freedom from the binds of the inner-void expressed by a state to enchant a sort of bondage upon the skilled worker who finds freedom in the technocratic and restrictive trades. I see that with the technological development of our present era, there is further some standard of task management gone awry, bribes replacing teetering onslaughts into otherwise perceived dire poverty.

In the chaos of the present era, there is order apprehended by the present-minded. The man or woman who can go soundly to the market brings with them the underlying truth to the nature of desire to bolster that very market. There is that power within the individual who gathers for him or herself some sense of duty to carry function within society, that the market bends to the woes of the needs. Losing the game it seems is only for those who give in to the temptations of the passive reality, to sit on the sidelines rather than argue to form, some feature and resolve to death. And if there is such a game of chance to further play upon the loss, there can be many players whom entrust upon us some scale to consider duty and behaviour et al.

The White Basket

In proceeding into a future of jobs and emerging markets, there is some justification to arguing for sustainable energy that the job front emerges more naturally. It is in developing a political theory to do with sustainable energy and the collapse of the infrastructure that the individual can find clarity amidst the bustle of new information providing us with a futuristic horizon of blight or common error. I see that modern political theory is developing to accommodate the job-seeker as is the state arguing on their behalf. This is of course by will of the individual to accept recursive assistance from the state, and there is that assured future thereby.

Manifesting a future of state prioritisation on behalf of every citizen, there is the extension to include differences between people by way of race and colour, gender and religious mechanisms enacting some degree of change as well. It is in the mutual assuredness of the state instigator however that the state as an actor better evolves to a model likening man to a machine. It is in our mechanical advantage then that there is a deliberate digression of ideas placed unto humanity as a whole, some higher vibration to the thing raising to meter. Aside from the current issues of justifiable duty to elect officials and appoint specific parties to offices that rights and free-speech are thusly insured, there is that argument that without a state there is freedom. The mind must argue boundary and it is there there is freedom within the bounds to fall to Her. Lux. The indolent.

The White Basket

In considering the freedom to act, it is within the scope of an individual's authority to argue justifiable recourse for every action upon the jest. It is in principal that there is due cause for objective certainty and with regards the investigation of raw data findings, there is bargain to master justifiable retort rather than counter-assuring the continuance of matters anecdotal to truth in purview. It is to the will of the people that the evidence of space is so tremendous that findings and considerations physical and mathematical are to be held to the luminescent bindings of all accounts due to the negligible differences in computer, verifying life to the permeated context of living by all justifiable means. That there can be life, there is that essence en sewn.

How can for the sake of citizenry one argue for the study of the ephemeris without considering the destruction of the pagan for his lack of printed effort? There is in the cross-examination of star patterns some course of viewing pleasure that the eye has not been obstructed by the subtle nuance of innovation, the glimmer of hope for recalculating our nearness to another star likening our propulsion to a match-igniter lycanthrope, that upon our resolve of the space current there is the measure of yield that all mass has accounted for leisure per event. Tragic is the work then that there is effort, there that blasphemy of the sciences at current a gross recant liable for the person harkening ownership over terrestrial affairs. That we are travellers and witnesses to the onslaught of societal events

The White Basket

amidst our selfish space travel, there is that encapsulating essence of the space farm that captivates the soul of the imagination to rally on behalf of technology to seethe. The future of mining in space those alien minerals is for better or for worse, the most industrial path to institute interplanetary travel therein.

We must wonder if the householder is prepared for such endeavours as making contact with a person or intelligence from another place. To have a proper environment, set up how we see fit, it is we are to consider the nature of the home before wandering to the skies to out-see it. Unknowingly for some parties, many countries rally on our behalf with large and harmful equipment to bring radio to the common gross. How are we to prepare our bodies for searches into the skies if we are not to raise to the higher light then without some army construed by saintly duff? There is that Star and common bond to erring.

Chapter 9: Self-worth

Should there be any hope to the development of a type of forecast to this life, that we have developed some science about the scope and future understanding of our life circumstances, I would praise such a person in such findings of such fundamental enlightenment should they be published. What a sage a person can be then, that there is that breakthrough in this life that grants us opportunity

The White Basket

to tune to the universe and live in the present to see our effective brethren form. How glorious of a life that would be, to sustain that presence about life which is so palpable at times - yet is so fleeting - the charisma doth nought. For many the many walks of people it seems, he higher-power's presence presents itself as a dangerous gasm of sorts, that there is that moment of revelry and boundless apprehension of light, a true scale to the hamper that grants us a resolve in this lifetime to assert the universe is infinite and boundless throughout it.

About what higher thing I speak is some presence that can be unhealthy. That soul-seeking Nirvana of the Hindu and Buddhist, there is that sense in the modern era that something of the old teachings was not lost, yet there is a trouble about presence I fear, that it cannot be sustained without physical effort. I fear that to endeavour upon the path of the relaxed meditator, there is an insurmountable depression that may present itself in kind. It is so sad I say this, as I have seen the scope of the emotion before so intensely, so subtly, and to the greater desirable effect, obvious, that I cannot deny the power of the desires any longer. It is that I seek the danger, yes, but feel compelled to address this mystical ledger sustain to the act. Perhaps in the challenges of the readership, there can be some sense of resolve about this mystical pretence?

As a matter of law, it can be postulated that the immediate witness to the heat is a sort of chemical instigator. It is the witnessing person who sees the cold of

The White Basket

the day, yet there is that conflict of nearness to the happenings of the tête-à-tête. The person concerned with only the mouthed occurrence is a selfish person, one connected through form ritual - aye - yet there is that feature lacking in the attempt to reconcile history that cannot be ignored to reduce the calendar to a store. It is the loss then to argue the gables.

People struggling for peace sometimes find few resources in the world to make large changes, relying on volunteer help and an exhaustive willpower of common writ. Animals become engrossed in the matter. But there is that essence inside of us that must unite to the event circumstances and accept responsibility for rightly action. Blaming the parties of the earth is useless to contend with the hugeness set before us in the skies. In dealing with time, there is that sorrowful aspect to time that we can make a material manifestation arguable to our circumstances, that the clock seconds tick by and we are found to be less foolish with each account of the moment we circle. We however as people must unite despite the nihilism to figure out the complexities of argument presented throughout history and our days ahead prepared for inaccurate tally. It is in the resolve of the moment we have seen evidence of the falseness to history's fables as well as acceptance and defeat of real-world ideations that science is hardly the highest aim.

Standing up to the universe is within our ability as humans. We can make a testament ring out into the void

The White Basket

that we are not alone. Aloneness it appears is in the aspects of our consciousness that beg to question inclusiveness to the universe about us we fare. We are enveloped by the universe to stand witness to it and make some claim within our lifetimes that Lux may take breath.

In realising the nature of another country than our own, it is imperative to expand the view. Howsoever subtle this view may be, we must expand it. We must reach out to the nature of reality to tally more than we believe we can handle. It is in our efforts to extend into the universe that there is a greater inclusion kindled. Even by our most lacking efforts, there is still the ability for the human to make adjustments to the realisation of the entirety of what this moment has come to be.

Let us again begin basic assessment of health and hygiene. Are we well-kept to proceed into the world where there is immense market and politics? Are we well fed that we have energy through the day? Are our clothes readily available to us should we desire to wear more or less? Ask yourself some basic questions of the health and concern yourself with this time that the nature of the world is heavy unto us should we fall to bizarre or scaled-out living.

Consider the basic needs of the human, that they can be met within this lifetime. Satisfy those urges that call to take care of the body. Is self-worth judged objectively from some semblance of order we have created for ourselves? Likely not. Consider the order you create for

The White Basket

your society. Move with that sense of order. Collect from it. Give back to it. Defeat it even.

In society, there is a course of honour which can be mostly unspoken but palpable. It is in taking action in society that one can endeavour upon a sense of dignity and honour, respect without inherent request for something in return. There is that living that can be that very fruit of desirable circumstance. Perhaps moments of recollection of history and staying up on current events is all that is required for some to adapt to this present time with enough will power to reflect upon the end of the day with pride. This pride is important, but it need not be mixed up with the racial prejudices of the past, pride associated with one's skin colour for example. It is in the course of honour and respect that one can learn pride, but it is usually short-lived. True to the nature of pride is in its callousness. We should remember this through our days.

In granting importance to this moment, there is the undeniable power of the catastrophe of the expanding and oscillating universe wherein we shine forth to do any number of just or unjust things. And giving order to our society can be an outlet to understanding the immense ramifications of having been born in our little place in the Milky Way. It is with great honour and accumulated sense of tact that I write to the audience in a way I am able to admit that I have committed some wrong, but in expressing myself I can only assure the reader that buried

The White Basket

deep within each of us is a sense of accomplishment and desire to settle the advances made against ourselves.

In having taught martial arts for many years, I know aspects of self control that some people simply lack. And it is in our desire to fulfil the feelings of power and commitment that we may find ourselves as martial arts losing control. We want to fulfil the kicks and punches and resolve that inner calling from the body that there is something in advancing ourselves upon others. It is in the control of writing to a readership at present that I find the most reward from communication of things martial and otherwise. I see that my days of martial arts training are mostly over. Now, my body will age. There will come a time when I see my body in space as an orchestration of both my successes and my failures. In considering my body ageing, I know that I have shown enough to this world thus far that my endeavours to continue to communicate by example will not fall short of remarkable. And it is this lesson I wish to impart upon readers, that there must be some showmanship to our skills and talents that they may manifest and make sound claim of our nature and spirit, if not for our prolonged survival outright.

In examining my relationships with others, I seem to have made grave mistakes in socialisation. And yes, it is I have given some type of advice in approaching this world. How can it be that I can reconcile my activities with others that have led to some type of failure while harnessing my more successful enjoining with others? It can be that we all

The White Basket

have our faults and I wish so deeply to express my sadness at the loss of certain friends and that it can be a reality for us. In approaching international politics, I have had a falling out with friends over the ideations of our society that dictate boundary of acceptable speech. I find that some countries do not prepare their citizens for certain speech indirectly related to themselves or others. But it only to certain scale I find this to be true.

In scaling our self-worth, it can be a hazard to confront the world based on the opinions others have regarding our sacred inner-self. For many of us living in the developed world, myself included, we tend to take advantage of amenities. When we do so, it is at times we lack a sincere exchange with others. We can take advantage of the easy access we as Americans and those of the developed world have in terms of communication and information. And it is at those times there can be much wisdom in arriving at a point in the lifetime where friends from various countries no longer apprehend us. Despicable self-aggrandisement on the part of certain Americans can cause rifts. And Americans are certainly known throughout history for both causing deep-seated issues and resolving them. So in questioning one's state, it can be important to examine such principals as self-worth and intention while keeping in mind that some relationships fall apart for unknown reasons anyway.

America is not in crisis. Should there be optimism before proceeding much further with publication on the

The White Basket

consciousness of the inner-man to march against the wills of the aggressors, there can be fewer important statements to support a *fact* that one's state is in crisis or not. Examine the state. Advance into that state. Look at it again. Are you responsible for social problems? Are you responsible for social change? If you have few answers to questions such as those to do with one's influence on the state, reexamine your place in that state. It could be that without a development in some type of relationship to a state at all - no matter how spiritually conscious or aware one is as has been reviewed - we could fall to unknown violence enacted upon us by crass authority.

In school I examined the Dalai Lama as a world threat. I studied the Tibetan *bardos*, those life-existences at, during, and after the time of death. I could not come to grips with the crisis of Tibet to be allowed to function as a free state given such intense views on death and religious material surrounding the procession of when and how life ends for people and what happens after we have been alive. I see that in examining Tibet, I have seen the crisis of growing to become an adult who can accept the totality of the invasion of China into the Tibetan Plateau as a sort of life-saving opportunity for Tibetans to develop alongside the free world. Human sacrifice. Wild-horse battles. Decapitations of Americans in the field studying Tibet. Tibet seemed to me to be an emerging threat the United States has tried to tame and assist as a state, but only to fail on some level in

The White Basket

supporting the Tibetan rights and freedoms. And it is perhaps in this extensive note on theosophy we may hem the parlay toward abuse.

In analysing a world power like China, it is important to remember the will. China is addled with social problems much like America, and following the trends of America, there are increases on attacks against Muslims and Islamic culture present within the Chinese State. China as a state *hack* computers as I hack computers for my country. It is such I find common error in the mistakes of Chinese censorship. One cannot ignore as well those animal rights abuses committed *to this day* by Chinese citizens. And yet, there is something about China that is undeniably beautiful for the developing world.

America has yet to gauge a force such as communism and its effect on self-worth. We reject communism outright, raised the way I was raised anyway. And for China to challenge marxism as an extension of communist doctrine, there is that aligning with an ally that was simply not present for America in certain countries. Cuba. The extremism of the Islamofascist ideations of muslim extremists. China is now accounting for problems America has analysed and gone to war regarding. And it is my hope there is continued relationship between America and China for those personal reasons of lessons learned between our mutual cultures. What would America be without Hong Kong and film throughout our industrial supremacy? Where would we be without mass immigration

The White Basket

of Chinese into the United States? Rail. Opium. Food. Paper. War. There are many things we've learned from China. And as an ally, our countries will grow strong to tolerate the misgivings of the religious instigators and no longer will we fall to a sin of common poetry - and oh how false the reality.

The Chinese state is immense its grandiosity and my notes on Tibet are that the socialites must reject works of art from the plateau. Art and music are two problems that will challenge the relationship between China and the United States and the future of the two countries rests in the balance of the finest discriminatory features of our self-worth and our work with state institution to instigate mutual suffering by way of legislation; China has suffered at our hand and will retaliate, but our lives are bonded through generations, that peace will conquer and mutual love and respect between Americans and Chinese *can* be real. Self-worth allows for that defeat of communism within the soul and reconciliation between our two countries is only a matter of time.

Chapter 10: The bad apples of radio astronomy

Picture if you will a scenario involving antennas that doesn't have anything to do with state livelihood or economic benefit. As challenging as it is to present concerns to a state, any easy way to voice a concern is with an antenna. A radio without an antenna has been

The White Basket

categorised by some as just a computer, but it is that theory of the antenna that presents itself for foreign nations and the reconciliation of the sciences. China's five-hundred-meter aperture spherical antenna presented in 2017 new discoveries that rivalled many findings in dealing with accuracy and student-to-government modelling in antenna use. It is in the Chinese model for antenna use by a state that we find a course unlike any other modelled in the world.

In assessing the moral foundation of those in charge of large antenna equipment, it is right to find that the choices of personnel made are to be contemplative for the householder. In exchanging currency with the man who holds a signal across his chest that an antenna-radio compels his wits, there is that sick man who beckons the health of the antenna with equalised dynamical feature about his body. A possible enemy. A rest-assured free policy of revelation or monitored use of radio antenna equipment, that thereby restitution is owed juris.

That there can be no noise, there is a rumble. There is a measure of a mark. There is that recognition of the pin-drop quiet in an instance, that the serving target has a height by diameter. There is that pinned instance that thereflood river per calculus emerges. There is that symmetry to the beauty of form and isolate that to absolve the molecules of the indignant repose, that to decay is to

The White Basket

residual some entropy noise ratio to fill. Can there be some sincerity in the signal then to tell us more?

Can the colour or distance change that to no production note short of critical there is a noir per every calendar? Can the skies not be calling with the noise of a hammer and yet we are still wrought with war? What is this North direction? What is this way that we have bent giving good deeds to magnitude to develop a system of navigation so heinous no residual calculation remains to tally the losses for the better part of a war with the gods? There is that fine line of writing the absurdity of our generation whilst avoiding the pitfall of disaster. Can there be some open book on the subject of foreign relations that the world could better get along.

It is in our foraging of radio signal data has come to exceed the findings of amateur scientists in determining who and where life comes from. We now know some bodies in space exhibit unique behaviour. When does the search for life become internationally warranted? Has it not been already presumed that the limit of our understanding of physics and radio antenna data has yielded little if any response from another world, yet we have made such bold star estimates that we smother the small amateur scientist in their pursuit of truth to the sky I fear, aye for I have a question. I would rather settle at being wrong about the access we have to scientific findings from large antenna than be obliterated by the poem of the woes of the English voter passing legislation amidst their

The White Basket

doctorate defence and a residual signal effect of some sort completely unrelated to the body, affecting the speech of a young woman perhaps, standing near a young man, the two of them together seeing no solution to the sudden changes in the rose petals fair introduced. Perhaps no story involving flowers manifests as a jaunt into a craft of a book of the art of the cabal but there is that writhing spirit that musters the intellect to summon the miscalculated guidance of a nymph, the work of an antenna. And it is in the raising of the arches that there is something better to the feet that impose a barrier to the solution about pain; that man and his antenna have reason, there is solvency in politics to subside that there is work.

How do we manage the antenna that present themselves to us throughout our burgeoning years of passing through the trials of these seasons? How may one accompany the surveyor that there may be mathematics implementation or short-sightedness altogether. It is without honour that I would seek a new measurement of antenna wire, that there may be some despicable factor, a change in the atmosphere. It works like this, to jolly ahead in the market with antennas and keep up with your area. Not to be too intrusive, but it is to the note that the end of the reel is so notable, there is no other way than to wander to the limitless quality of uncertain characteristic that the psychology is distempered. That is to say there is that psychological roughing-spot that may be suitable for the permeating broadcasting man that plays and displays

The White Basket

flutes and other colours for his killing-kindness to Plato, that over the frequencies of the antenna he doth not play.

There is that essence of a man who challenges the better residual impact layering of another algorithm exchanged by another man and yet there is that tempting shielding of the features that one knows about the wits of the play. This is all to say there is no antenna greater than the moon. Yet, with all the dandy way about it I find it such displeasing that the Island countries have not rallied for experimental use quite marvellous as Great Briton to move the damn thing. The lunar impact on the maths theory has yet to really take shape.

In his lesions against propaganda, our own Prince Andrew awaits the beckoned call for his antenna that it is berated to orgasm amidst the crowning Virginia. Aye, what a sexual Charles. Our antenna discussion that I divert to the celebrity as Jodi Foster, it is in my deepest sincerity that I see such a woman as Jodi struggle with the Mormon, that the National Security Agency team Utah cannot possibly rally, this is but some false aspect of the pectulescent imagination. I see that the use of words to describe the antenna gasm and shock of this planet have resulted in some of us being pitted to be close together in our times, but as Mormons, I cannot claim that there has not been but every Mormon life lost to any antenna of the land given how many free electrons the datacenter has held oh-so-devastating(ly). It is in the proposition of free speech that a man is allowed to act as though interned by his bed

The White Basket

gasket - a procedure of Lux, the carelessness. There is that sincerest jester arch in the bow manifestation of true form some colossus as an antenna to grant ye false speculation amidst the grander of uniform triangular spherical inset-lay of the most common appetite, to the likings of a common construction worker should such an occupation see fit the antenna to stand in the economy; this is to say that there is a man left with a penis functioning to its minute that he may urinate yet not be gauged by a signal in his bowel. And it is this impure man who builds an antenna.

We as human beings have been forecasted a blasphemous and prideful remark in the uncaring assemblage of persons to judge the works and accounts of physicians, machinists, and common-tucky of the kindfolk that might ordinarily conjugate with one another to the free bedroom if such slack might concern the rebellious outlooking Russian upon examination to do ill health to us. Speculative is then to say that there is not for every equal of a man, an honour to do bidding to some spite about his rainbow; that Celtic inner-soul manifestation must resound as an arching triumph that a man has made claim to his bedroom and fit upon his head some rhythm of the blood of another man before yet another stands to claim a signal has penetrated the dihedrals of the Utah stone to disturb the celebrity obsessed with making alien contact. This is to say there can be no mandatory gay. Nay. Absolute is the vector for which there can be some true

The White Basket

resolve to point an arrow at the fact of life such as this, the life free from same sex interactivity that there may be sound maths, that all deterministic sequences are a line. And that for every angle, there is one motion the moon has ever made that no neanderthal will ever once more claim upon this earth some kind of jagged anal manoeuvre to a vegetable or a steak before the grade of food is judged by the distance from the porcelain to relieve the negating spirit of doubt as to the possibility of life in the stars. There quite honestly are those sequences as those that should otherwise lay to rest in another publication's overdue mortgage bust operation of a dug-out sophisticated plan of man to every action of the corner of a room, yet there is that soul that within us brokers to an antenna that we may politely calm the wits, freeing our minds of the suspicious intricacies of the universe. There is that unallowable agitation in our family plot that cries out when correspondence dodders and we have fallen out into the field and have involved ourselves with extensive antenna, yet be that man who he is who is quality to not regain agitation to the bane - be a person once more to call to the antenna of your dreams I say. Call to that antenna. Study it. Make it a longterm feature on our hearth.

To the drinking words of the acquisitions of the small fitchets, there is that raising of the narrow gobstopper to the residual abundance that proclaim any open mechanism to the grandiose turning of space, be my enemy. Be my reconciliation that an antenna broker hath

The White Basket

doddered a relationship to manifest for me some rightful place in the palace should I show enough strong wit and mechanism to remain upright, I am without fitness it seems in my waking, that I may be enamoured with desire to take the rebuttable so far as to instigate sorrowful suffering on the feature of a man in his thirties - myself. But there once was a civil path where I declared an end to my possession of high-powered antenna. And the magnets. My how the ozone swarmed at the magnets, claiming the lives and opportunities of the neighbours should the military or police have any just say about a thing to do with the wrong deeds committed against my fair republic at that time. Oh, as it has been cast out from this midst, a great pang, this rejected antenna forma we come upon, that there has been fair discussion with the ghost ensemble that there be some presence in the equipment high-gain register? Argue that there is a burial for a man and a slant to his angle that his lower back muscle hath not higher-vented some circumferential distortion of means. This higher beckoning to the patriarch is that there is a perch for every meadow in the countryside should not some slumber occur where might one insert the curious antenna to the anus, per se, that there is some measurement then of the relation to his penis to the show the earth. This should be such a hilarious folly to have happened already, interpreted as star plot coordinate to somewhere in the university mind you. But fable be felled oh so Chelsey - that to give in to the breasts is another mention of the nipple,

The White Basket

there is the callousness to undress the hands for back-paddering, spanking the bottom. This is to do away with any unnecessary radiation from our dream antenna of choice, mind you, and that fable that the scientist has transcended the power of the rocket once more shows in the bowels of the fletching tyrant. This is to say there is another antenna for our liking elsewhere than here perhaps. And with that, the doctorate must rekindle the fires of amazement elsewhere that the journey is befit for a teething of pulses between the armlets so jest with parle that a Wallsmith and a Fox could not pirate one to the Jonsdittor of Iceland in her Poetry. But she hath been named, so Chery - that she is not hip to some party twerking of Harry's dinger and the folly that ensued in the Merkel affair some doctorate contest? Nay. For there is a shadow of two men who play but the music of their days for the journeys. And the antennas have. To say this in pause, this is that some malfunction of the very science of naming characters as yet to manifest so unruly as to answer another poetical digression. Where is the box spring beneath our formal mattress to select the woman to the bedchamber instead?

    Should a man or woman journey from their cavern where they stay, oh and should they agitate the socialites as many have cried of late about whom I shan't write but naught, and yet, there is that lasting effect to the antenna broker still that cries out to some absurd wisdom. There is a mechanism of an olive branch of some sort within the

The White Basket

companies one so mindless in acquisitions would argue, but there is prudence in the constant mis-measurement of antenna and the fixture that accompanies the absurd result of the two-day angle, when all pitches resonate to an occurrence. There's only one of them apparently, and we have sworn we've spotted it, but the science conjecture is out on antenna magic by the time any absolutist has ever found time to assault the key terms.

It seems more doctorate investigators are required to keep marring the insides of the canister that the National Security Agency stays strong in its defence against Germany. We must be shielded from the devastation of the Merkel fallout in her campaigning for doctorate level violence, and we see that her happy cunning as a world leader has not absolved her of any due responsibility for propagation of the master plan and its far-witted analysis of key points and lectures on the aneurisms of past lecture upon book upon table upon obsolete. May there be a new term. This has been the Germany of my yearly fables, and my propagation of pronouncements to do with antenna have yet stripped me of my right *none* in saying that there is some resolve to the distemper of the Austrian speculation should some degree the Czech wear the uniform, adhering to American digressions of the television for some better and progressive view. This is to say that the magic of the Slovak has not died of uniform baldness in its psychology to appeal to the networks of the emboldened Oprah and Dr. Phil - in continentally

The White Basket

misaligned technical zoo-patterns of scattered out madness about nazis and soviet tanks shadowed by the American hype. We have more freedom now to argue the misgivings of what we should take to the table should there be drama so happy in our lives that we cannot share a religion like the Mormon has to his wife. Have I in some way married the women of the reich then to my flavour that Merkel and Theresa May cannot stand together naked in the shower? This is to ponder the suggestive oversight required for breast exam without barbiturate weight-training to set the standard higher than the Norwegian that Merkel battles Down's Syndrome to the grave as honorary principal to her word. Yes, then I say there is that collusion of our most grand antenna, when there has been a cherished moment unlike any other female Prime Minister than She that cat's meow of Downing Street, oh' Beloved Theresa May almighty Maidenhead this period, that she has written to us. Cannot any audience have seen her displays in the house of commons than to realise the utter spectacle of personable honour that had collapsed upon my American lungs whilst studying the Caldera Yellowstone than to have realised there was a female prime minister at all? Now, to the grand refrain of the Obama Administration, it is that the National Security Agency has had to release that pain and anxiety of not knowing once before where that scoundrel Snowden may be, but should he so advance his readership that there may be an incredible weight released from his shoulders and he is offered safe return, there can

The White Basket

be no shining moment than to ask him personally what *he* would have done to Theresa May if *he* were to have allowed in some pious light Theresa May herself to assign Merkel as the Queen Her Majesty that she may take procession in the house of commons by incident most tragic her English, then it is true I have seen the power of an antenna collapse. And Snowden. Where do we resolve that poignant remark on the balance play of journalism to strategic advantage to subterfuge the National Security Agency Germany Journal on Open Tactical Warfare Mechanisms Against Germans? Where was Snowden then?

    I was certainly at work with the instigation of another paragraph to praise the pi-specialist Daniel Tammet's gross negligence into Iceland none than to remember the joy of America's Joe Rogan rocking over onto a microphone to play spat to an NSA half-wit employee who contracted *himself(ie)* to the journalistic West that some nature of the fruit of Mexico should not slide any more a bullet North toward my direction when wrangling the crass Mormon Zetas of their cartel houses. What then of Snowden in his crass attempts to bend the intelligence to say he has served? We should ask, where were you when I drove through Russia and back without not participating in a fake crying episode over satellite to Vladimir Putin's judgement-microphone small-boy Soviet hatwater of a smile at me that I was driving some two-hundred miles per hour on a highway with Yokahama

The White Basket

himself laughing from Japan? Snowden. Small potatoes. When America opens up, life is revealed.

Where we leave off with a picture like Snowden is in wondering when does he commit a crime in Russia so worthy of press he has any earnings? We must wonder for the individual who hath so prestigiously left us, yet it is that I too have left me family to settle somewhere else and work for a while. I do not wish any modern harm to come to the man mind you, but I still see some recollection of the nature of sin in a man who does not have courage to stand for his country when it is subject to banter and ill-witness. Now, in continuing this bullshit ballpark National Security Agency gang assault of Edward Snowden in our thoughts, our hearts, and with a USB thumb-drive in our anus for Khrushchev, there is that dishonour to the field that cannot be argued as claimant present in tithings to the United States to have served our own interests through calamity. That is Snowden has so closely aligned himself with the draft he could be some mystical ally to nowhere for the Soviet Union to freely experiment upon. But his rights and freedoms restricted to pen as they are, it is understandable there will likely be little fallout from the tragic sufferings of Snowden's inner crisis to resonate with the modern party. There is certainly no lack there that a man has shadowed another in his job and seen the spectacular error in his divine judgement that he should cast upon a man to say to a young man, from the Russian Federation, to his face - "do

The White Basket

not honour a man. Do just as that man." And nought to be shot. To say Lenin grows on us is to do as a marxist does in panic upon confronting the marxist denial of the holocaust that some land as ours has been shafted from a distance of yet another hardcover release of a book by an American to lay claim to a territory wherein he inhabits, it is there is crying in the field, and the old buck journeyman whom have wondered near and far to testify to the insanity of finding Edward Snowden, only to appear to him as a confrontational tribesman holding some standard of advocacy for the Native American. In my mystical folly I can only believe Snowden has casted his doubts on the media enough that he is ashamed. He has little reconciliation to gather and his publications will be daft. Should the hard working young men and women begin to set to book their service and their time served, it should be every technical equal ready to read the markings of those who have served.

In testifying before congress should there be any witness testimony from those whom have ever colluded with the likes of the Utah gang of National Security Agency high-tech Mormon society: gay, straight, black, white, and feisty high on drugs by prescription to serve this country, there are stories. And we hope only to read between the Bluffdale, Utah lines drawn against Maryland should we be hip to the glory of the NSA.

The White Basket

Chapter 11: The instigation of a legend against the almighty

It is in the habit of every creature that there cannot be some resolve to do crass witness unto the environment that circumstantial evidence of an effectively dead enemy is not some enemy that has not stricken the lines of a failed system enjoined unto him through poverty. It is in reconciling the war dead that a man may then argue to his estate that he has no enlistment of slaves unto his matter and that his life may proceed forth. It is in deploying such a canister of truth unto the matter of deploying the right propaganda into the battlefield that there can be a strategy against poverty that is acquiescent of administrations prior without doing harm to the current seated president, and yet there is that untold necessity to ignore the current presidential matters in their respective Manchuria.

I see that the tip of the rifle is at the bore of the youth that have been laid to waste in their nascent adolescence than can possibly have been sustained by an ecosystem without significant evolutionary pulses in our cycle to not argue some insurmountable destruction unto the environment to prepare for one's own wake. And yet these kids, but a generation behind ours, they have lacked some rebound and recoil of a continual purveyance of transgression about instinct that there is not some loss to the youth recognised in the soldier. I see that the men have witnessed enough service - many of them to have retired

The White Basket

from any economy of the functioning empire at current, ye our youth are spontaneously argued to fight. It has been without recent exception that there are words strewn about by generals concerning the liberal youth and their undertakings, but it can be that the common intelligence operator is a witness to that key social change already that a committee can not be raised into place to suffice for inaction; yet it it is by some standard of the human frame to sustain the hard-wrenching youth holocaust of a loss of a soul for another and not remember the child-like look to the crying eyes of a solider who keeps some memory of his sibling on his person in the battlefield. I see that there is that aiming of the missile, that there is some instinctual look to the interpreter who sees that youth are ganged and collied by insurmountable fears and troubles. What I fear is the heavy handed digression into parenting that our future generations are not prepared for war at home once more, that the war on the frontlines of the home stretch of the last court served against Hitler isn't yet destroyed - well, there is that special place in the American soul about the disaster of the Chinese state in its brevity to annex the Manchurian settlement ounce more, but there is more strife than paranoia in the muscle of a man with a gun pointed at any world leader in his thoughts to not ring out loud at least once some shot in the dark - a fantastical bullshit no-place to nowhere. The flat out nihilist lie of our elders as shown us that modern technology reveals itself to the true believer of the word upon the stretching out of

The White Basket

skin over soothing rice paper to argue in some category an adjacent idea to another stretch of ever-so reaching to the pissing lines of Generals upon stacks of dead bodies high worth of paperwork some recollection of spirit for a strong Navy. And I see that the boats still sooth the burning skin of the civilian in the hope that some poor rich subservient to the Bermuda Triangle not reach the epitome of all costs and argue for himself some yacht on a credit line to Prince Andrew's cum for Virginia herself, well then there is a mistake that has been made. Prince Andrew is hereby to retire from the public life and the royalty are to be investigated.

In finding and honing in on a decision being made that risks an imbalance to the overall temperance of a particular profession, there is that establishment of refined posture to mock the insolent broadcasting spirit of a man, that there is some loss to the affect or feature in war that a man's recognisance has been lost before his eyes with an ordinary checkup - and like that he's on no drugs of his or her choice. This I argue is the death of a state, when a man has a choice to do drugs as a soldier to defend his country yet, it is likely in his dishonour to take drugs to intoxication, he has recklessly ruled out the duties of his life in some way that the needs of the state cannot be met. Thus, there is a drug in development to insure a task force can bare witness to the scope and monstrosity of the scale of the orderly procession of the most illegal chemistry. And only fitting

The White Basket

that in theoretical organic chemical writings is there some juris to the matter of intoxicated state of residual molecular cohesion that some pages have yet to bond in the succulently *used* hardback or leather edition for further chafing, there is that daft recognition in even *attempting* to publish chemistry as I have that some downdraft of the room strikes that it can be finally that your own family holds in their hands some of your own science to the likeness of your prior handling. Nay. It is that all chemistry is then bound by the state to be enacted upon the mere mortals, those state enemies that reside therein.

In drug policy for changes for the state better, there must be some acceptance of the reality that the amateur scientist must derive drugs and identify toxicity in the blood, else there is that fear of the transfer of the Chinese organs in the state, that such terrible happenings do not lay claim to so many beings without being accounted for in the most simplest of outline. Can not some sympathy for the children factor that morrow be their fascination in the wrongdoings of their elders?

Cannot there be some state that settles for the Indianan that soon there is that respite against the constitution that claims hemp can be the greater communist arrow than the clever drug consumer in his herrings to do injustice against a householder by consuming in a way unlawful to that state? Can it be that the challenges amidst intoxication of the householder to maintain his workings are such that illegality is not the

The White Basket

moral bond to the root of a crisis on instigation of law rhetoric in his favour to give due sovereign appeal to his community to resist the workings of law enforcement and yet there is some higher English statute that gives mandatory prudence to enter this man's estate and take him from house and home upon the death of his family members by sheer cause of nature alone mind you, and yet we have few law arguments sustained in our capitol given the abandonment of leadership on the part of Vice President Mike Pence to leave the state for the rushing-on of the Trump Administration and yet *still* there is exhaustion to give credence to one person living intoxicated in the population who commits crimes against animals. There is one executioner per every law that can be argued to sustain life under Pence, and now there is this freedom. When will our state bend to find acceptance of intoxication as necessary to hold house? For it is so that one must partake of the communal draw that there is a well, so shall there be implementation of law to make cannabis lawful under Trump Administration guidelines. The thread of Indiana is strained and we are ahead on malnutrition and must *appeal* to international law by our day else there is no light. May there be a promise in Brexit that our flag shall reign as the Georgian does that our stars meld against the capitol. There must be this resistance to accept cannabis to the state efficacy of acceptable by product use and development as such issues as propaganda and tithings to the authority of war calendars must be

The White Basket

argued that all persons of Indiana are set to malnutrition under draft and are thusly ordered to the war schedule of the Trump Administration. Our state is simply unfit.

That leadership within the state legislature has failed medical board effects in clause in such a sophisticated means that laser eye surgery is challenged before implementation of recreational marijuana laws defines for Indianans what the dealings of Chicago are to meld for the regional forecast against claims of slavery and bond to the southwest as residents of Indiana as some argue to vote, there must be some allowance of the free householder to dismember his cattle amidst the joyous bounty of cannabis smoke. Yet it cannot be leathered some task to the tanner that laser procurement for iodine is found to be chemically inert in the state of Indiana to a drug task force centred on criminal law reform. It is justifiable then that any doctorate must rise to a pulpit in some written form to advocate for some "celibacy from the drug" that certain language be argued that particular counties mostly dry from alcohol refrain from postage of signage indicating alcohol to be available on a particular day, there is the sun. And that is the effect of the farmer's apprehension that he may see the glass window of a door that reaches across his britches to his wallet before EBT and Wick are challenged for minor drug offenders. And should there be such law encroachment upon the farmer that there is task to the land, then it is to blot out the skies with weather modification before Senator McCain in his

The White Basket

Jesus-resurrected great glory grace the Alaskan skies to bare witness to the divorce of former governor Palin herself - by task that he lay witness to the sacrament before him, this woman - and taketh his dead hands away. The McCain doctrine grid implementation failed under Pence and failed under McCain, just as the general as a man who proceeds in law to do some journeyman act against the folds of his local law courts upon returning from battle, so too is there misjudgment of the offender. I see fit that there be some release of information into our community of DNA evidence that can produce itself as intoxicated - which is to say *pro bono* - that there is not some writing on the subject of challenge to the phenomenal acceptance of a farmer to refrain from role as householder and maintain the life of a slave instead that one instance of prescription medication go left unchecked for one day for one resident per ear of corn. This is called a market of sodomy and it is by constitutional law that the farmer has at random before him any account of drugs of the community for free rights experimentation. What right then is there that a resident of the state of Indiana cannot stand as witness to testimony against the state as a whole body acting in the ways of South African apartheid in such slaughter of the hen? Can there be some argument that the farmer has transcended some action of the machine mechanical that he is not be born of food or prepared in an emergency for a communal roast should he fail in his share cropping? This is a question of the legislative branch of government that

The White Basket

resigns itself to a mysterious office of county court and is some fictitious body of free-will arguing patrons to the hallucinatory affect of no effectual state inquiry without the lame attempt at the hen; that every man is taken from his community before federal implementation of vaccination not be granted to every pain-free slaughter of an animal and nay will some arguer of Seattle, Washington grant me a rainy day for a psychiatrist to declare me unfit for duty to declare war on Russia once more, that oh hail Mary may the blood and the sacrament reign down upon the royalty born here then. Indiana is the strictest state of the Union and has rightfully deified its governance to province by *proctate* thus we rule as a land does *not* apply to this winnings here this day this bread. It is that the food of our air must be born of might and the hemp crop has proven strong enough to be sustained under the weight of multiple men per machine, thus it is the cause of the pharmacist to call to war the local resident in arms against the farmer that taketh to task the tractor so violently there is upheaval of the meal. That is that any medicine so worthy of anti-nausea is to be free-will acceptable to a community for communal use. It has held to the bathroom before that marijuana is a crime and that no writer within the state should attempt let alone to any international standard to generate a word-mass comparable to some argument as to allow for recreational marijuana by forced tithe as seen by MKULTRA. There can be only the wish of a child to remain sober that no drug be forced unto him. And thus the nazi of

The White Basket

the state rises to contemplate sobriety under laws which ban the distribution of marijuana and its pornographic glass that is better suited for the dildo than be acceptable in a school. How never we learn these glass arts I have seen in a shunned Taiwanese citizen of the United States who argued before me hand-blown beauty of a mastery of that illegal work-ethic under the law to have inhaled his materials on the job-site. It is every smoker then who is responsible for constipation but Reagan's failed implementation of nutritional supplement by inhale-able means led only to a sort of legalised methamphetamine used in over-the-counter inhalers to this day. There is still that stigma of a nutrient that cannot be breathed. I say we *must* take in some intoxicant of the lungs and that should it be by smoking I should die, then I have been a compatriot of the Lucifer sin. Heroine-free and supplemental to the opiate sunlight. What then does this mean? Does this imply that Lucifer holds law over Indiana and its schools? Indeed it does, but for the working man and those clever to have enacted rule changes for the clever.

To see police intoxicated and working under the power of prescription drugs and radio duress without proper assessment of field-use of improvisatory antenna and radio for the benefit of educational demonstration to Federal Communications Commission versus federally commissioned rail property appropriation of athletic trails for duty fitness (on and off duty), it should be by forced implementation that all on-duty police officers of the state

The White Basket

of Indiana and abroad be fair enough to compel a bike alongside a firearm, that is to question his partner in his uneasy caution about the roads with him or her while still compelling to radio some chime. And bicycle use alongside firearm training is thusly permitted to enact the Australian madness of state failure unto the Indianan by further enforced exposure to a firearm pursuing every open path the bicycle "may random." That is that there is at any one time a man rides a bicycle one act of avionics in his favour for supplemental assurance that there is a distance North he may fare is vertical rather than horizontal to his plane. This is the inception of flight and the mechanical propulsion of remedied flying machines yet to be loose as our fair dealings with drones will shadow the rights of every investigator to take ownership over the laws of a plane. That every resident must declare law in his or her lifetime to maintain state residency as an Indianan, still there is the democratic wanderer. And the centrist of the Trump Administration promises to work hard against the wishes of Lucifer's great enemy to any woman of any age to marry that the sharia law of Michigan in its Dearborn be of any waste to the kindness of the state legislature to pass beef, there has not been plain riddance of the armed Seventh-Day Adventist in his Texas ramblings enough to legalise bicycle marijuana habits - naturally. It is my some mechanical gesture that we must still go to war unfortunately it seems, and against the muslim this season will be yet another turning in the great soviet cocoon of states once tried and tested for the implementation of communism. How grand? Perhaps a mandatory walk to Mackinac Island? Laws have been passed before.

Chapter 12: Merry Christmas

May there be a gift shown to this earth born for the lives of those who have lived, may there be *The White Basket* to draw a lattice to the truth of the seasons. If there is something I have learned from Thailand and the acceptance of a basket for seasonal religion if not in form of the *Pali Tipitaka* of the Theravada, it is by some Luciferian deceleration unto man that there be born a set of laws to implement free gasm to benefit from a celebration of Buddhist tomes. Such language in alchemy would relate my tithings to Ra's sun god under Ma'at's sincere direction, her scribble patches of palm-leaf-bereavement of Sheshat's great arms, there can be only the understanding that the Thai buddhist has offered me something called the Phra Buddha Chinnarat, the most beautiful golden buddha of Thailand that weighted-standard of gold has to offer by way of measurement, mind you. There is nothing like the Phra Buddha Chinnarat, particularly when it is handed to you as a gift for your reeking intelligence to do with Buddhism. And I have argued the term to a misspelled happenstance of torn apart law armies of small men gathered in shaved head uniform under a buddhist psychology of the *Abhidhammatta Sanghah* to stand ready

The White Basket

against the United States and Hitler. I have given them a book entitled *The Book of the Oculus* and it is supposed several monks are on a journey to infiltrate the Indian army and procure for me a jet aircraft for every head the Indian at auction. It can be then that I possess many many things and would kindly turn over my acquisition of subsequent military craft to the United States should I be at lot internationally and unable to defend. I have yet to fly with an Indian and I speak only in mild fable to retain ownership over the sincerest volume of my writings without the Bihar School in authority for generations not to be raised by some Thai argument of the theosophist. Grant me your ears about the celebration of the Thai for the holiday?

I would like to see a maintenance of this grand holiday al Christmas to celebrate the happenings of the beauty of the developments of the Thai state that their newly drafted constitution be held above the heads of the slave-women who serve as unduly difficult concubines in their remembrance against the state aghast in the drama of late. And I see fitting that the King of Thailand visit the United States to greet my President, whosoever he should be. Thus shall it be that Senator Elizabeth Warren is not to trouble Thailand the matters of the Thai Queen, should she be so palindromic - as there is a Thai word for such a thing - in her Japanese. She is to me to greet Shinto Abe in his rad excellence that there is a new bridge to our South and North with the full acceptance of the Japanese Staff, his

The White Basket

"on-footedness-that-he-purveys-as-emperor-to-be" as there is a word the Yakuza have argued for the benefit of Elizabeth Warren herself that she should hold such common threat as the senate against the navy of japan in her failings to rise to presidency. Such common threat as false weather from the Thai navy and Warren would falter at sea I argue, but only for the betterment of her safety as an American in raising confrontation of women's rights or gender studies with the Thai - and to our Thai naval policy that the boys upon the boat play as the girl form he may be, yes shall the democrat be gay and marry. Thus there is a Thai constitution and it is to be placed at the burial head-chamber of every Indian Buddhist, but only in meditation. There can be no reconciliation of the way the petals have fallen for martial arts of Indonesia to not have influenced Thai dance. Thus there can be no more consort. And her journeys must yet again rise within the Thai epic of the unspoken girl in the song, that there be honoured by Thailand this Japanese emperor great - and there is fine peace in Asia once more.

May there be a Thai merry Christmas. How can it be that the United States can give gift to Thailand when she has honoured such much gold that Bhutan is but a legend in the colossal mis-measurement of luminescent male feces to suffice for gold on plate this Thai maiden, that there cannot be a type of seasonal deal that the United States allows for the tour of the Phra Buddha Chinnarat with some Thai-specific machinery? Cannot the imagination of

The White Basket

the chemist argue failure to the Pali books of righteous oversight should our United States constitution compel but the nascent Thai to write? I ask should there be such a machine to lift the gold in weight without specification as to its mass that there cannot be a Thai woman who takes the land for the failure of such a machinist set to task to lift the Phra Buddha Chinnarat in all his colossal efforts to not turn the gear as a Catholic. Perhaps the Mormon gears of the ephedra can inspire the spice of living for the fair trade of the Chinese back to his ancestry before Thailand venture to drift the Phra Buddha Chinnarat at sea however, and it is should be argued that in the air is where it is fit to travel... then, but only then. For the Maharishi Mahesh Yogi has an Iowan corn solution for failure, and that is a simple mattress upon exhaustion of such a thing that there is Thai-stick, i.e. hashish. But, can a consort propose such a squanderers' tale as to lift the Phra Buddha Chinnarat from its place after all?

It is once more some issue of drugs to do with Thailand that we have not acquired more of their stunning aircraft through theft. Bhutan comes to mind in considering how best to treat the lower legs of my kickboxer student of Thai origin, that I would muscle through and break his delicate feature to a maim and no match for the rest of his school career. I consider in training with him that there must be an infernal distance between the two of us yet we know each other to have succeeded at arguing the Buddhists face-to-face about the

The White Basket

realities of their nazi offerings, though for some Thai children the monastery though it looks hip when captured in photographic standard, there are others that fall to the tithings of the sea-born mystical entities we do not see in the buddhist literature acceptable from Thailand, writings subsequently lacking visibility in printed form within the States. And where to travel for such literature can be ofttimes that illegal sanctuary of the boy's palace. It is where he plays with his cellular telephone and is naked about his peers whilst too humiliated not to saunter off into a life of drugs and monastic-Theravada fusion - and I worry for him. It is in the dangerous Thai rituals we do not see as the West that there is often great inner transformation of the most pristine linguist susceptible to brutal kicks and punches of the kick-boxer should he fail to argue the Thai canons.

In the the japan hard submarine is a fleeing South Korean dressed as Kim Jong Un. For some time a new emperor of Japan must take a stance against the Thai nation. But within this round of the colossus of the Japanese institution of high art and discipline most electronic, there is but a Chinese shattering blow to arms and negotiation between the United States and Japan that cannot be resolved through Korean influence. I consider then in my parsings, though I have have such absurd reverence for the maintenance of Thai Pali language in the monastery to consider Malaysia and the failings of certain *Nei Kung* principals to have not better migrated to such

The White Basket

regions as to have not come from a violently affluent Indonesian set in his ways. And I see some wisdom then to the fighting of boys in the Thai monastery where cured Indian cow testicles are served as a pious delicacy. Though forbidden knowledge of Thailand is technically illegal and must be argued with some keen stat-li-hood in mind, I see that the Thai physical law on the transgressions of the Universe are fair and comparable in defeating Kant in the early-most primary to not ascend to doctorate quite quickly that the Thai body does not age much from fighting. Thus there is peace in Thailand we do not see. And this is most lethal. It can be compared to an absurd samurai sword act with some Japanese melon over the stomach of a nascent and noir-tense student of the failed Indonesian kris science of exorcism.

Thus it is Lucifer must come to erring. There is once more that the Christian has ordered Kant to the surgery floor before removing the book from the fire that reads Nietzsche's name from the affluent householder's fire pit about some radio field generated from filth. Difficult in recollection of the source of all gasoline as the the pineal function argues for an Arab cigarette is some consolation that the lessons of Asia are well masked in the science of the devil. It is in our keen observation of the emergence of sophisticated language that can be observed in the arguing of the other finer baskets of Thailand, some basketweaving insult by the father to the likeness of, so long as it holds to a degree, there is the buddhist who has remorse for the sick

The White Basket

Christian dogmas of the Thai import of a type of mysterious fascism of the Moon rhetoric with such party habits as MDMA drug-taking and full-contact martial arts as being acceptable for the Thai person. Such sadness. And still there is that slant into North Korea viewed as bombastic and showy, aye, and there is that rise to the North Korean mountain where there is the sudden glimmer of North Korean photographic development of the simple picture of a leader for the Thai youth who desires to standardise in the personal application of makeup and somewhat detestable modification of the colour of the iris by means most crude to optometry, though expensive and well-justified regardless of fascist or depressingly Asian for our youth to be troubled by the hazel beauty of the natural boy. Aye, there is that sentiment about the nature of Lucifer that argues quite heavy to law to protect the beauty of the asymmetrical Thai in motion. I fear for Thailand and pray very much that there is sustained acceptance of her Island in mercy that any fat tourist takes a picture for food and small women that they balance to forfeit in their bullied recklessness as students. I cannot accept that my own knowledge of Thailand which is quite private and much to do with women in higher social order be not better broadcast to a diplomat than shelved by a skeptical antenna monger from some dangerous Vietnamese import. A person who simply does not exist.

I argue that there is no remaining Thai nihilism inhibiting some part of punk-rock conversation in the

The White Basket

wildness of the science attempting to remedy Thai drug addiction, for there are abuses here. The drug-taker can argue with law enforcement some better approach than the death penalty so long as there are few actions which lead to violence - one would hope - and it is howsoever sad to see the death of the Thai people to their own arms in such brutal implementation as an armed buddhist reich standing against Hitler. So I see that the monasteries must close one day.

In closing I hope for the best for our planet this season. With climate change having a severe impact on our human conscious perspective in ways obvious and subtle, I foresee that madness about the spiritual and scientific will stabilise. Though our families about the Earth bicker for space and as wars between countries continue to be averted, I fear for the Muslim of the Hui and his future. Theosophy has stricken about the world the many works of religion and it should be to the responsibility of the remaining theosophists and anthroposophy in his architecture and education to recede from the comings of the science. It is however that in our spirit to maintain the many religious and philosophical tenets of the world and contest our limitations with scientific bounds, I see optimism in the peace about the matter. Dear reader, work hard to stay alive in these trying times.

The White Basket

Acknowledgements

I would like to thank my family and the United States government resources for all their efforts in assisting me with my healthcare needs and resourcing. I would like to thank the many hearts of America, Yemen, Ukraine, England, Russian Federation, Uzbekistan, Romania and China ... the list goes much deeper; I would like to thank President Donald J. Trump, President Barack Hussein Obama and the many federal employees with whom I have had correspondence; I would like to thank my attorney and the hard work of local police and fire fighters; I would to thank Richard Estep of Her Majesty's the services for his endless patience in teaching me to make the hard decisions. Hail to the Queen and Godspeed.

www.ingramcontent.com/pod-product-compliance
Lightning Source LLC
Chambersburg PA
CBHW030713220526
45463CB00005B/2029